SEARCHING FOR NEVER, NEVER LAND

NEVER LAND

A MEMOIR OF BEING LOST AND FOUND

JOHN LAND

TWS PUBLISHING

FOREWORD

The more things change, the more they stay the same. Empires, cultures, families, and individuals are on repeat—same song, second verse. We seem to learn nothing of history, and so we keep repeating it.

Two thousand years ago, the Apostle Paul stood in the Areopagus and proclaimed the Truth. He told the men of Athens that the "Unknown God" they worshiped was the very One who gives life and breath to all. That same God is no longer unknown. Love Himself has been revealed in Christ Jesus—closer than our breath.

Woah. A mere fifty-eight years ago, I was a boy running through the woods near Andover, England. With my friends, I was swinging from vines and sprinting through the forest when something beyond the scope of normality happened. My body snapped back mid-stride, then upright again. I stopped, heart pounding, and retraced my steps. There across the path was a strand of rusted barbed wire, neck high. It would have taken my life in an instant. I should have died that day at twelve years old. And yet here I am. Had I too encountered this Unknown God?

Now, buckle your seat belts. You are about to enter John Land's amazing journey. You will walk with him through searching and restlessness, and later in life, the voices that threatened hellfire but never held the final word. You will be immersed in the '60s and '70s of sex, drugs, and rock & roll in San Francisco and Northern California. You will travel to Hawaii, where Eden turned to chaos—organized crime, brutality, even murder. And you will wonder how anyone could survive.

Time after time, year after year, decade after decade, John was aware of a Presence. A voice, a shadow, a hand on his life. No matter how far he ran, no matter how deep he sank, the Savior never abandoned him.

This book will cause you to look back upon your own journey and see the handprints of grace as well. Whether it is an apostle standing before the history-makers of Athens, a twelve-year-old boy spared in an English wood, or a man named John Land searching for *Never, Never Land*, the message is the same. Love Himself is present. Closer than your breath.

Trust me, dear reader, you will never be the same.

WESLEY TARPLEY
AUTHOR OF *OPEN TO MYSTERY: EXPERIENCING THE ANCIENT OF DAYS THROUGH BREAD, WINE, AND POETRY*

ENDORSEMENTS

John Land's *Searching for Never, Never Land* is a raw, unflinching journey through the spiritual wilderness of the 1960s counterculture that ultimately becomes a powerful testament to divine grace. With remarkable honesty, Land takes us from his childhood encounters with an invisible "Friend," through the psychedelic haze of San Francisco, the supposed paradise of Hawaii's communes, and finally to a Christmas Day revelation that changes everything. This isn't just another come-to-Jesus story—it's a masterfully told account of how God pursues us even when we're running in the opposite direction.

Land's vivid prose brings to life both the beauty and brutality of the era, from transcendent moments on Mount Tamalpais to violent confrontations on the Kona coast, all while weaving a deeper narrative of a *Presence* who never abandons him, even in rebellion.

What makes this memoir extraordinary is Land's willingness to expose his failures alongside his searching—the abandoned family, the broken promises, the misguided pursuits—without excuses or self-justification. His story reminds us that the God who saved him from drowning in Ocean Beach's massive waves is the same One who meets him on a Filipino church floor fifty years later.

Searching for Never, Never Land is essential reading for anyone who has ever wondered if they've wandered too far to find their way home. Land's journey proves we are never truly lost when Love Himself is doing the seeking.

DR. BRANDON VAUGHN, AUTHOR OF *LOST IN CHRISTIANESE* AND HOST OF *ADVENTURES IN GRACE* (RADIO AND GAN TV) WWW.ADVENTURESINGRACE.ORG

Searching for Never, Never Land is a captivating memoir of my father's extraordinary life, blending a profound spiritual quest with tragedy, misjudgments, and adventure.

From a psychedelic awakening on a mountaintop to the chilling reality of being targeted by the mob, to living in a volcano crater in the jungle, this book pulled me in with its vivid storytelling and raw honesty. I had planned to read it over a few evenings, but once I started, I couldn't put it down and finished it in one riveting sitting.

A must-read for anyone seeking inspiration through a wild journey of self-discovery, spiritual survival, and finding that invisible friend who is intertwined with mind, soul, and cosmos.

MALACHI LAND IS A 43-YEAR-OLD ENTREPRENEUR FROM SANTA CRUZ, CALIFORNIA. RAISED WITH THREE BROTHERS AND A SISTER, HE HAS BUILT A THRIVING BUSINESS IN NORTHERN CALIFORNIA WHILE SHARING TWENTY YEARS OF MARRIAGE WITH HIS WIFE, NICOLE. A PASSIONATE TRAVELER, MALACHI HAS EXPLORED THE WORLD—FROM CANADIAN ICE LAKES AND WEEK-LONG WILDERNESS TREKS TO CLIMBING MAYAN PYRAMIDS IN BELIZE—CARRYING A LOVE FOR ADVENTURE THAT RESONATES WITH HIS FATHER'S INSPIRING JOURNEY.

———

What a joy to read a book written by my friend John Land. I could hear his voice and recognize his personality on every page. The stories I had once heard in pieces came alive here in vivid detail, and I finally saw the whole picture of how God pursued him— from his restless youth to his miraculous encounter with the Truth.

Though John's journey is very different from mine, I found striking similarities, especially in his freedom from depression at the moment of conversion. His descriptions are so potent I felt I was experiencing the events with him—even wincing at the pain of the beating he endured. Beautifully written, this memoir has everything: suspense, adventure, personal turmoil, and deliverance. I couldn't put it down. Other books I was reading quickly lost their place.

What a gift John has given us in this story. I look forward to book two.

JOEL COOPER IS A RETIRED PHYSICAL THERAPIST LIVING IN BAKERSFIELD, CALIFORNIA, WITH HIS WIFE, DEBORAH. TOGETHER, THEY HAVE A DAUGHTER, AMANDA. A LIFELONG SEEKER, JOEL HAS FOUND REST IN THE FATHER'S ETERNAL LOVE, THE SON'S FINISHED WORK, AND THE ABIDING PRESENCE OF THE HOLY SPIRIT.

CONTENTS

NOTE FROM THE AUTHOR

I'm writing from memory. More than fifty years have passed, but I've done my best to tell these events as accurately as I can. This account reflects how I remember the key events from my childhood, adolescence, marriage, and my time in Hawaii from 1971 through 1974.

This is a story about an awareness of a loving Presence and my journey to find out the identity of this mystery that touched almost every aspect of my life. The words of an ancient Catholic saint, Julian of Norwich, perfectly express my feelings about the invisible Hero of my story—Someone who was always there and never failed me:

"All shall be well, and all shall be well, and all manner of thing shall be well... For there is a force of Love moving through the universe that holds us fast and will never let us go."

That force of Love pursued me until I finally understood who —and what—real love is.

John Land
CALIFORNIA, AUGUST 2025

PROLOGUE

My story begins when I was eight—when I first sensed something unseen, a Presence beyond the natural world. I couldn't name it, but I felt it. At the time, I accepted it without question. As I grew older, that quiet awareness became something more—a hunger, a need to understand. That hunger would eventually drive me to abandon everything I once knew, rejecting the safe, suburban world of my upbringing for something wilder, something real.

By the 1960s, the world I had known was crumbling. The middle-class dream—the promise of America, of family, of faith—was unraveling before my eyes. While we played baseball in the streets and mowed our front lawns, the country was being torn apart. Racial riots set cities ablaze. Political assassinations shook the nation. A senseless war sent teenage boys to die in jungles they'd never heard of. The Cold War made nuclear annihilation feel inevitable. And then came the moment that shattered America's illusion of innocence—John F. Kennedy was shot, and we were told to believe the official story.

For my generation, it was the beginning of a mass disillusionment. College campuses erupted in protest. The music shifted from feel-good rock and roll to anthems of rebellion. We no longer trusted our government, our institutions, or even the faith we had been raised in. Everything that had once been sacred—God, family, patriotism—was being ripped apart.

After a four-year stint in the Air Force, I dove headfirst into San Francisco's rock-and-roll scene—a world of music, drugs, and revolution. I turned my back on my grandma's Christianity, completely rejecting the 'bloody cross' and everything I'd learned in Sunday school. I was searching for something deeper—truth unwrapped from what I believed were the lies of Western ideology.

I looked for it in the psychedelic haze of the counterculture, in the music, in the Eastern mysticism that promised enlightenment. In 1970, my favorite San Francisco band, Jefferson Airplane, released an album that became my personal manifesto—*Blows Against the Empire*. Grace Slick didn't just reject Christianity—she tore it down, sneering at its two-thousand-year legacy and calling it a fraud.

It was a battle cry—an upside-down, broken cross for a banner, a rejection of everything I had once known. And I was ready to burn it all down.

I wanted truth. Real truth. And I was willing to go to extremes in my search for it.

The ancient Greek philosopher Plato wrote, "The worst of all deceptions is self-deception." I didn't realize it then, but I was about to step into the very thing Plato warned us about, and I couldn't see it. I was blind. Like Mr. Toad from *The Wind in the Willows*, I plunged full-speed into my own wild ride—ecstatic, reckless, ultimately destructive—racing toward a private hell I mistook for freedom.

But before the riots and the protests and the long road away from faith, there was a boy with a creek, an oak tree, and a friend no one else could see.

PART ONE
FOUNDATIONS AND FRACTURES

"I didn't know His name, but I knew His Presence—always there, always saving me, no matter where I turned."

CHAPTER ONE
SOMEONE WAS THERE

I was a quiet kid—more of a loner. I had a younger half-brother and a little sister, Tim and Karen. I loved them, but truthfully, we weren't as close as brothers and sisters ought to be. Solitude suited me. I rarely joined the neighborhood games—not because I was disliked or without friends, but because I didn't care much for what most boys seemed to chase. Sports never came easy, baseball least of all. So while the kids played ball in the street, I slipped off to the woods and the creek that bordered our little tract in the northeast corner of San Francisco Bay.

Those woods were my kingdom. The creek was alive with mud turtles, stickleback minnows, bullfrogs, even crawdads and garter snakes—everything a boy could wish for. Oak, willow, and buckeye trees leaned over the water as if they'd been planted just for climbing. The air smelled of bay laurel and wet earth—sharp, mysterious. When I startled a covey of quail, the sudden explosion of wings felt like magic.

Home didn't feel like the creek. Affection was scarce, words of love even scarcer. But out there, among the water and trees, I belonged. The woods and valleys, creeks and hills—they felt like mine alone.

Even as a boy, I sensed Someone behind it all—not the far-off sky-God I heard about, but a Presence closer, kinder—a Friend. I didn't know who He was, but I knew He was there.

In my favorite oak, I'd lie back on a limb that fit me perfectly, as if it had been made for me, and talk into the open air. Sometimes I talked about my feelings, about what was going on with my family, and whatever was on my heart. Sometimes I asked questions I couldn't ask anywhere else. I never heard a voice back, but I always sensed an answer. So much happened in that oak tree —so much listening, so much wonder—that I never once felt alone. Someone was there.

I followed the deer trails so often I could've walked them with my eyes closed. What I really wanted, though, was to see a big buck up close. They were always just ahead of me, just out of reach. One afternoon, on a narrow path, I whispered like I always did, "Could I see a big buck—up close?"

I wasn't testing or bargaining. It just felt natural to ask a Friend.

Right then, a huge buck exploded out of the brush beside me and landed on the trail a breath away. We both froze—me with my mouth open, our noses touching, all muscle and stillness. It couldn't have lasted more than a few seconds, but it felt like time stretched thin. Then he sprang and disappeared.

I stood there, heart banging in my chest. The deer was amazing, sure—but what stunned me was the quiet certainty that my whisper had been heard. Someone had answered. I didn't have a name for Him yet. But He seemed to know mine.

I'd caught a tiny ring-neck snake—olive back, bright orange belly, a beautiful, soft ring around its neck. Smooth and quick in my hand. One day, it slid through my fingers and vanished into the grass. I looked until my knees hurt. Nothing.

Days later, I was mowing the lawn, still thinking about that little snake, and I asked—quietly—"Could I find him again?" I wanted that snake so bad! A few steps on, I stopped to pick up a scrap of paper so I wouldn't shred it with the mower. Under that one small piece of paper, on that whole big yard, was my snake—coiled like he'd been waiting for me.

People can call it a coincidence. Maybe. I only knew that time and time again I was seen—even in small, silly boy things. *Someone* was there, answering before I even knew how to pray. And that left me with a question that wouldn't leave me alone... *Who are You? And what do You have to do with me?*

I also kept pigeons—tumblers and homers. I loved opening the coop and watching them climb into the sky, wheeling and tumbling, flying free. Something about their freedom stirred me deep inside. But what amazed me even more was how happy they were to come home again—to their nest boxes, their eggs, their squabs. It's hard to describe, but those birds brought joy into my life that was real.

I wasn't trying to be spiritual. I wasn't sitting cross-legged hunting for the meaning of life. I was just a boy who loved being outside, watching water find its way over stones, listening to the woods breathe. But still—there was always a Presence. I couldn't see Him, couldn't name Him, but He felt as real as the wind on my face. Sometimes I wondered if I was making it up. But then something would happen, and I'd know—I wasn't.

As I got older, I didn't talk to my invisible Friend as much. The woods still called to me, but my days filled up with new adventures—surfing the northern California coast, shaping boards, chasing waves, chasing freedom. The oak branches and deer trails of my boyhood started giving way to pounding surf—freedom of another kind, one that carried its own danger.

It was 1964, and my surfing friends and I were at Ocean Beach near Golden Gate Park in San Francisco. That year, a massive storm slammed the California coastline, bringing historic flooding and some of the biggest surf the West Coast had ever seen. The waves at Ocean Beach were enormous—so powerful that at high tide, the foam and whitewater washed over the seawall and spilled across the Pacific Coast Highway.

The waves were deafening—frightening—and irresistible.

Unless you've surfed big waves, it's hard to understand the attraction. Only a madman would paddle out in that kind of surf.

At Kelly's Cove, a legendary spot at Ocean Beach, some of the waves towered 15 to 20 feet high. Paddling out through the violent shore break was almost impossible. The waves never gave an inch, pounding you again and again as you fought to reach the spot where the rideable waves broke over the sandy reef. This break had no channel to paddle out into the wave. You had to charge the shore break until you got through.

After what felt like an eternity of pounding waves, I finally broke through to the lineup. I say "lineup," but I was the only one out there. And looking back, I know why.

A set rolled in, bigger than the rest, the first wave steepening fast. My bravery outpaced my skill. I took off too late. I was launched into the air, then the wave swallowed me whole. Everything went black.

The water was frigid—54 degrees, typical for the Northern California coast—but I never felt the cold. I didn't feel anything. My board washed up on the beach, badly damaged, its wooden stringer bent like an accordion. I didn't wash up with it.

I was gone.

The world went silent. No light. No up or down—just water pressing in.

I was somewhere underwater in that violent whitewater. The sea foam generated by the surf was several feet deep, and it was impossible to see anything floating in the water.

My friends searched the beach, scanning the surf, waiting for me to surface. I never did. I had been under for too long. They thought I was dead. They were about to call the Coast Guard. And then—impossibly—I washed up on the sand in a massive shore break wave, deposited like a piece of driftwood on the sand. My friends ran to me as I came to—very much alive. Coughing up salt water and sand.

The undertow should have dragged me out to sea. The violent whitewater should have held me under. I should have drowned that day.

But I didn't.

One moment, I was lost beneath the waves, swallowed whole by the sea. Next, I was coughing up saltwater on the shore, my friends shouting my name. I had no memory of surfacing, no struggle, no desperate fight for air.

It was as if I had been placed there—saved by something or someone beyond me.

I knew it wasn't luck. I knew it wasn't chance. The ocean should have taken me. But it didn't.

Again, my invisible Friend answered a prayer I never prayed. He pulled me from the deep, just as He would again and again.

At the time, I didn't question it. There was no room for doubt. It wasn't luck. It wasn't just the force of the waves. I knew. Even before I could fully grasp what had happened, even before I could process how impossible it was, something inside me whispered the truth. He was there. He had always been there.

I'd known Him in the oak tree. Now I knew Him in the undertow.

I didn't say it out loud. I didn't have the language for it yet.

That moment on the beach stayed with me. Not just because I survived, but because something I couldn't see—something I couldn't explain—had pulled me from death. As a boy, I believed I was seen. As a young man, I knew it.

I wouldn't have said it this plainly then, but it's the truth I can see now: I was never really on my own, not in the creek, not in the oak, not under the wave. Somebody had their eye on me. Somebody kept stepping in.

The current wouldn't be the last to pull me under—but neither would it be the last time He would save my life.

After that, life kept moving. School. Work. Weekends at the river. On the surface, it was nothing but forward. Underneath, something was shifting. The country was coming undone, and we were about to be swept into a decade that would test every belief we held.

The 1960s were heating up, and I was right in the middle of it — though I didn't yet know the peril I'd faced in the surf was nothing compared to what was coming.

CHAPTER TWO

A WORLD COMING UNDONE

Growing up in the turbulent '60s wasn't easy. The longer I lived through it, the more it felt like events just kept coming at us like violent assaults.

At first, life across America looked safe. Kids played ball in the street until the lights buzzed on. Dads mowed lawns and waved at neighbors. Moms called us in for supper. On Sunday mornings, the streets emptied because many families were in church. Flags hung on porches and pies cooled on counters. And in the Bay Area, it had its own flavor—new tracts of homes were being built everywhere, freeways and new factories, an excitement that life was good and moving forward. And for me, the nearby ocean.

But even then, beneath it all, you could sense a current of tension—subtle, but growing, waiting to break the surface.

When John F. Kennedy took office in 1961, it felt like a new chapter had begun—hope wrapped in a slim, confident man. I was thrilled. Kennedy was young, sharp, and forward-looking. He spoke with a confidence that made people stand taller and dream bigger. The whole nation seemed ready to follow. He talked about reaching the moon, about peace, about making America strong— not just in the military but in mind and body.

By the following year, when I entered high school, you could feel the energy everywhere. Our school even joined his 50-mile hike challenge. Most of the cross-country team did the first 25 miles—me included. My legs were wrecked, but who cared? We were full of hope. My friends were full of hope. The country was brimming with it.

Then the world shifted—at first just a change in the air you couldn't quite name. The headlines started carrying a new edge, as if every story was darker than the one before. Something was off, though most of us went on pretending life was steady. Maybe we didn't want to notice. Maybe we didn't dare.

News came in October of 1962 that the Soviets were hiding nuclear missiles in Cuba, just 90 miles off our coast. They called it the Cuban Missile Crisis, and the name alone sat heavily in our chests. The whole country panicked. People stocked up on canned goods and water. Some talked about digging bomb shelters. It felt like the entire country was holding its breath.

At night, lying in bed, I wondered if we'd all be gone by morning. If a nuclear war were going to kill us.

And then—Khrushchev backed down. The missiles were removed. We all breathed again. Kennedy had stared down the Russians and won. For a moment, it felt like he'd saved the world.

But while we were watching Cuba, another front was quietly opening. In 1961, Kennedy sent a handful of military advisers to Vietnam. Just a few at first, quietly, without much fanfare. It didn't seem like anything that would touch our lives. Vietnam was a distant place we barely thought about. But the gears of the war machine had started turning, slow at first, then faster. By the end of 1962, there were 11,000 advisers on the ground. What began as a whisper was becoming a steady drumbeat in the background of our lives—one we didn't yet realize would drown out everything else.

Even as the threat of nuclear war began to fade, trouble was bubbling back home—rooted in an even older struggle. In the early 1960s, the civil rights movement was gathering force. Sit-ins spread through lunch counters across the South. Freedom Riders challenged segregation on buses and were met with mobs and firebombs.

The nightly news was full of the civil rights struggles of the Freedom marchers and the violence and murder they endured. It electrified the nation, forcing America to face injustices we'd ignored too long.

In 1963, Dr. Martin Luther King led a march in Birmingham. Peaceful marchers, elderly, middle-aged, and teenagers—some not much older than me—were sprayed by fire hoses and chased by dogs. Those images invaded every living room in America. And once you'd seen them, you couldn't look away.

That August, more than 250,000 people gathered in Washington, D.C., to hear Dr. King deliver his *I Have a Dream* speech. I watched it, glued to my television. I'll never forget it. His words rippled over that crowd and into the heart of the nation, lighting a spark of hope again.

Then came November 22, 1963. Dallas. The motorcade. The shots.

I couldn't believe it. None of us could. Not JFK. Not in America. In a moment, the hope we'd felt only months before was shattered. Everyone alive that day remembers where they were. I know I do.

The silence afterward felt enormous. Adults looked at each other like something unnamable had split open the country. It wasn't just grief. It was deeper—like a hole had torn through the center of everything we thought we knew. I wanted to ask my invisible friend, Why? But I didn't even know where to start. It felt like every family, every person I knew, was carrying the same raw question in their chest.

The weight of Dallas lingered, heavy and raw. We all wanted to believe the worst was behind us, and 1964 would steady us. But before we could catch our breath, the next blow landed.

The Civil Rights Act promised equality, yet that summer in Mississippi, three young men were murdered just for trying to register Black voters. Freedom wasn't free—it was still costing blood. And I couldn't stop thinking about the families grieving their sons and daughters, cut down for daring to believe America's promises.

By the spring of 1965, the anger erupted in Selma. Peaceful marchers crossed the Edmund Pettus Bridge and were met with clubs and tear gas. It was on TV for the whole nation to see—men, women, even clergy beaten in broad daylight simply for wanting the right to vote.

That summer, the new president, Lyndon B. Johnson, signed the Voting Rights Act, pen in hand, calling it a great step forward. But days later, Los Angeles exploded. Watts burned for nearly a week, and suddenly the smoke wasn't just in the South—it was right here in our own backyard.

It felt like we were all waiting for something else to break. You could sense it building but never knew when or where it would finally give way. And still, reeling, we didn't see how fast the following shifts would come.

Also in 1965, Johnson sent thousands of Marines to Vietnam. The death toll kept climbing. Boys barely out of high school were being chewed up in a jungle we'd barely heard of. It was sick. I was frightened.

I joined the Air Force that year, hoping it would spare me from the worst of it. Thousands of us did. Boys just like me—barely out of high school, the ones we'd surfed with or run into at the beach on weekends—were being sent to fight in jungles they'd never even seen on a map. And for what? No one had a good answer.

At home, everything else was unraveling too—riots flared in the South, then California, then spread town by town. Smoke billowed above neighborhoods that had been peaceful just days before. College campuses turned into war zones—students linked arms, pushing back lines of police, their voices cutting through the hiss of tear gas as it drifted across the quad.

It was an era that marked us all—chaotic, volatile, unlike anything we'd ever known.

Meanwhile, the war kept growing from a few advisers to over half a million troops by 1966. Each night brought a new casualty count from Vietnam, another city burning, another headline about corruption and betrayal. Each one chipped away at the country we thought we knew.

Sitting in the barracks one night after hearing about more riots back home, I closed my eyes and tried to sense that invisible presence again. "Are you still there?" I whispered. "Does any of this make sense to you? Because it sure doesn't to me." That presence I'd known as a boy — it felt so far away. But sometimes, in the quiet, I'd feel it again. Not loud. Not clear. But real. A flicker.

And in that flicker, I felt less alone—as if maybe the same presence I longed for was holding others too, families, protestors, soldiers, in the middle of the madness.

This was my generation. And I was a perfect product of the madness that marked the '60s and '70s. It wasn't just about the war—it was everything. Injustice. Inequality. The lies we'd been told about who we were. The American dream we grew up on—steady jobs, safe streets, neighbors looking out for each other, clear lines between right and wrong—was collapsing before our eyes. The heroes were dying. The government was lying. The war was endless. The streets were on fire.

Kennedy. Then King. Then Bobby. One by one, the lights went out, and with each loss, the darkness grew heavier. Patriotism became a joke. How could we keep believing in freedom and justice when the same country that promised equality was turning its back on its own people—and sending our friends to die in a war no one could explain?

Each headline, each image of violence and grief, chipped away at what little pride we had left. The "land of the free" looked anything but. The dream we'd been sold—of unity, justice, and freedom—felt like an illusion. It felt like chaos reigned, and the country had lost its mind.

And as the Vietnam War raged and racial tensions exploded, I remember thinking: we've all gone mad. The whole country has lost its mind. It's no wonder we ran. Some into protests. Some into drugs. Some into movements, music, rebellion—anything that felt like freedom.

Me? I was still wondering if the unseen Presence I had known as a boy could be real in a world this broken.

CHAPTER THREE
SHATTERED ILLUSIONS

It was 1964, and on Friday nights in Richmond, MacDonald Avenue came alive. We piled into our cars and cruised back and forth, over and over. Windows down, tunes blaring, the night felt easy. Just cars full of teenagers, like us, just trying to escape, showing off our rides, waving at friends, maybe catching the eye of a girl at the corner. The hum of engines, the chatter from sidewalks, the smell of burgers and fries drifting from Foster Freeze—it was our weekly ritual, a little escape from the heaviness we all pretended wasn't there.

Nothing extraordinary, just an American teenage rite of passage. For a few hours, it felt like life could still be simple. It was the kind of thing that gave us a break from the world outside—everything that was on the evening news, everything we couldn't make sense of. We could forget it all for a while. Or at least we tried.

But that night, something changed. It wasn't just another

Friday night. The tension that had been building, the anger, the fear—it found us. It became personal.

Sixty-one years later, that night is still burned into my memory.

I was cruising with my friends in my 1954 Chevy Bel Air—just the four of us, rolling along behind a line of cars making the loop on Main Street. The usual crowd. The usual Friday-night buzz.

But then the line of cars stalled. Engines idled. Nobody moved forward. At first, we thought it was just traffic—the usual bottleneck when too many kids tried to make the loop at once.

I rolled down my window to see what was happening. That's when I saw them.

Hundreds of Black people—of all ages—were rushing down the street, smashing windows, setting buildings on fire, and breaking car windows. They dragged teenagers out of their cars, beating them senseless. The mob was wild, fueled by a rage I couldn't fully comprehend.

In the car just ahead of me, they shattered the windshield and yanked a boy out onto the pavement. They beat him mercilessly, slamming his head against the curb. There was blood everywhere. I don't even know if he survived.

At the time, I couldn't process anything beyond raw fear. But now, looking back, I wonder how long his family carried the unanswered questions, the grief. For me, it was terror and escape. For them, it may have been a wound that never healed.

We froze. My car was next. There was nowhere to go—no place to hide, no way to escape. Nobody said a word. The air was electric with fear. We braced ourselves, expecting to be dragged from the car, beaten, or maybe worse.

And then in a moment that seemed almost unreal, the Richmond police flooded the scene. They appeared in riot gear, with truncheons raised and police dogs snarling at their sides. The mob that was beating the teenager's head on the concrete curb was suddenly set upon by police dogs.

It was brutal. Horrifying. The chaos, the screams, the violence—it was like nothing I had ever seen. But in the chaos, it was also the only thing that kept us from being next. Relief and horror sat side by side.

In that raw moment, it was a terrible kind of deliverance. My car was spared. We were spared. Looking back, I have no doubt my invisible friend was there, too—the same *Someone* who had saved me countless times before—intervening again that night. He was my savior, once more.

At the time, I didn't even ask the question that seems so obvious to me now: Just my savior? Why us and not him? Maybe the shock was too much. Or maybe my teenage brain didn't know to think that thought. What I do know now is that time and maturity can help with some questions—but not all of them.

But the shock of that night never left me.

Until then, we in White middle-class America had lived in a bubble. We thought equality was being handled in courts and Congress, far away, something the nightly news covered but didn't touch our lives. We told ourselves everything was fair, that opportunities were the same for everyone. But that night on MacDonald Avenue, the bubble burst. It wasn't a headline anymore. It was blood on the curb, rage in the streets, fear in our own chests.

We weren't outsiders watching unrest on a television screen

anymore. It had climbed into our cars, stared us down, and left us no choice but to face it.

After that night, I couldn't cruise the same streets without feeling the weight of it. The laughter at Foster Freeze felt thinner, more fragile. The world was shifting under our feet.

It seemed like the normal middle-class society of the 60s and 70s was being turned upside down and torn apart. When reality clashes with your closely held beliefs and illusions, the results can be devastating. Everything—*and I mean everything*—was changing, and it wasn't comfortable for anyone.

The streets felt different after that night—like innocence had been stripped away. And the songs on the radio started to change too.

The carefree surf songs gave way to protest anthems. Guitars turned sharp, restless, trading love songs for cries of anger and hope. My generation's troubadour, Bob Dylan, spoke for the '60s generation as we rebelled against everything that seemed patriotic or moralistic in our culture. How could they moralize against my generation for psychedelic drugs, free love, and a desire for peace when they were guilty of mass racism and sending us to die by the thousands in a senseless war? We were shouting with the counterculture revolution: *I want peace.* I want nothing to do with your wars, your hatred, your prejudice, your middle-class bubbles... *or your God.*

It wasn't just music—it was a mirror, held up to a generation trying to make sense of the madness.

I wanted to believe the simple world of Friday-night cruising could last, but deep down I knew it was gone. If childhood had been a safe house, the door was off its hinges now. Nothing felt steady anymore. And no matter how hard I tried, peace seemed out of reach. And I wasn't the only one. All around me, my generation was starting to look for answers in other places, chasing freedom wherever it could be found.

What had once felt so solid—America, church, even my invisible friend—suddenly carried cracks I didn't know how to name. And if the world outside was coming undone, so was the world inside my own house. Shadows I couldn't escape were already shaping me.

CHAPTER FOUR
SHADOWS OF THE PAST

Mother was usually distant and cold.

At seven, I was told never to call her 'Mama' again—only 'Mother.' The word felt formal, sharp, like a wall between us. I don't remember hugs or warmth or the easy sweetness I'd seen in other homes. Visiting friends, I marveled at how their mothers laughed with them, actually seemed to like them, and they seemed glad to have them close.

What I knew instead was the sting of criticism, the deep pain that whispered I could do nothing right. She made it clear I was more of a burden than a blessing. That feeling of not being wanted lived in my mind and shaped everything—my friendships, my sense of belonging, even my worth. It was a phantom always at my side, whispering, "You're not good enough."

And yet, I loved her—more than I knew how to say.

It took me years to piece together the weight she carried. My aunt Dimple's memoir painted the picture: Arkansas, the 1930s.

My mother was a little girl dragging a cotton sack down rows of white cotton, her fingers bleeding from sharp bolls. Her father drank away what little money there was. Her mother—the one steady figure—forced the girls to church every Wednesday and Sunday, as if faith alone could keep the family from falling apart.

The men drowned their shame in bottles; the women carried the scars. One of my mother's sisters nearly lost her life to a drunken husband who tried to strangle her. Another fled with a child in tow, running west toward the shipyards in California. My grandmother followed with her daughters—my mom among them. They left Arkansas behind, but not the hurt.

That kind of pain doesn't vanish. It seeps into you, reshaping how you see love, how you hold—or withhold—affection. My mother carried it all. And without knowing why, I carried it too.

She married young—sixteen—a handsome Marine corporal named Everett Weston Land. I was born a year later. He was gone soon after. She never healed from that abandonment. Every time she looked at me, she saw him.

When I was in the third grade, I finally asked about my name. We were in the driveway under the peppercorn tree when I worked up the nerve. Everyone else was Montgomery. I was Land. Why? She told me that Bill Montgomery wasn't my father. My real father's name was Everett Weston Land.

That was it—the conversation closed. From that day on, she never spoke his name again. The silence did the talking.

She refused to answer questions, as if in her mind he didn't exist. She hated him, and maybe that's why I often felt like she saw me as his shadow. To her, I was a reminder of desertion. To me, I was just a little boy who wanted to be loved. Growing up a Land in a family of Montgomerys only deepened the ache.

But even in that silence, something else stirred. As a child, I felt Someone close—unseen, yet unmistakably near. Not the far-off sky God I heard about in church, but a Presence that felt personal. Kind, yes, but the deeper question haunted me: *Who are You?* That mystery trailed me into my teens and beyond. I didn't know His name, but I knew He was there—answering me before I even knew how to ask.

Years later, my Aunt Millie slipped me a picture of Everett. I looked just like him. That photo was a treasure and a wound. It left a great empty spot. Not knowing my natural father was hard to carry.

The Woodson women's history with men shaped everything. Abandonment and betrayal ran like a vein through their lives, and my mother carried that fear all her days. She could never forgive Everett Land. The wound he left never closed, and I think she took that fear and suspicion out on me. From the time I was born until she passed, she just couldn't risk opening her heart to the danger of caring, loving, and then losing. It crippled her. She never knew how to have deep relationships.

That fear turned into a kind of coldness she could never shake. But I never stopped loving her. I can't say the pain and rejection didn't follow me for years—it did—but I understood where it came from, and somehow that gave me the grace to look past it.

It took decades before I saw her soften—even at the very end. But I did see it. The wounds didn't have the final word. Grace did.

Still, life had its lighter places too. Summers meant Steamboat Slough on the Sacramento River. A camp trailer under the cottonwoods, the smell of suntan oil, engines droning as skis carved the water. Mother loved to camp, and Bill loved to pull skiers. She always reminded us it was for her enjoyment—not ours

—but I didn't care. It made her smile, and that was rare enough to treasure.

Those river days felt almost like a truce. The fights and coldness back home receded, at least for a while. Sometimes I brought my friends up for the weekend—skiing, camping, laughing by the fire. During the week I worked, but the river was our escape. At night, when the camp quieted and the water lapped against the bank, I'd lie awake under the stars and feel that nearness again—the same unseen Someone I had known since the creek and the oak tree. The question pressed harder then: not whether He existed, but *who He was* and *why He cared for me.*

Most weekends outside of summer, home life was so unpleasant that I found reasons to be away. Granny's house. An aunt's place. Cousins. Anywhere the air felt lighter. Books were another exit. I read like I was starving—Robert Louis Stevenson, Jack London, Hemingway. Adventure stories where boys became men, where danger was thrilling, and the world was wide. At night, it was Ray Bradbury and Isaac Asimov—science fiction that felt like prophecy. Alone in my bed, flashlight under the blanket, I wandered other galaxies while the real world kept its distance.

Jack London's life hit me hard. He didn't just write adventure —he lived it. Alaska, the sea, hard labor, and rebellion. It lit a fuse in me. His life was just as wild as the stories he wrote. I knew then that I would never be satisfied with a boring, humdrum existence. A deep craving stirred in my soul. I wanted to experience everything that life had to offer, not just read about life but really live it.

I knew in my heart there was something more—a world where Someone existed beyond what I could see, feel, or touch. Just thinking about it felt like both an adventure and a reality. I say *reality* because time and again this unseen Presence showed up, leaving me with no doubt He was real. What I didn't yet know was His name, His identity. That was the mystery that pulled me forward.

CHAPTER FIVE

THE BREAKING POINT

The tension in our house was suffocating. My stepdad, Bill Montgomery, and I couldn't agree on anything, from the smallest details to the bigger issues—politics, work, even how to live life. We were on opposite ends of everything. As a journeyman electrician, Bill got me into the electricians' union when I was 17. I worked the summer as an apprentice at an oil refinery, but what I saw on that job left me disillusioned. I watched journeymen electricians loaf around—putting in hours for a paycheck yet doing nothing productive. When the company complained, the union rep threatened a strike to shut them up. I couldn't hold back my disgust, and I made the mistake of sharing it with Bill.

He was a staunch union man, heavily involved in union politics, and he lost it. He told me I should be thankful the union "took care" of their workers. That was the last time I ever worked a union job. Bill made it clear that if I were going to be too high and mighty to support the union, he'd make sure I never got another

union job again. To me, it felt like a betrayal, and it drove a deeper
wedge between us.

My junior year of high school was an emotional and painful
time in my life. My mother and I were fighting frequently. It
seemed that nothing I could do would measure up to her image of
who or what I should be. It was obvious that she saw me as a
failure and made sure she reminded me of that fact often. I loved
my mom and needed her to love me and approve of me. I was a
competitive swimmer in high school, competing on the varsity
team. In four years, my mom only came to one swim meet. We all
need a mother's love. It shapes you—whether you know it or not.
The thought went deep into my heart that if your own mom
doesn't like you, then who could?

During that dark time of overwhelming sadness, the invisible
presence I had known as a child returned to my life. It would make
itself known again, somehow, in a way that I couldn't ignore.

I was going steady with Jeannie, my high school sweetheart—
she'd eventually become my wife. She gave me the emotional
support and love that I was craving. We were inseparable after
school and on weekends. I spent a lot of time at her house, often
helping her babysit her youngest sister, and I was a frequent
dinner guest. My life at home was falling apart, and I leaned on
Jeannie for the love and acceptance I couldn't find at home. I
needed her. Looking back, I know it was my own selfishness and
insecurity that drove me to depend on her so much.

Then it happened. Out of nowhere, something I never saw
coming. One day after school, we were sitting in my car when she
told me she wasn't sure she loved me anymore. She had doubts
about our relationship. Her words hit me like a physical blow—

hard, swift, and crushing. I felt the ground beneath me shift, like my entire world had just been pulled out from under me. A deep, black hole completely engulfed me. The pain was sharp, raw, and overwhelming, as if everything I had held on to was being ripped away. I fell into an abyss that seemed endless. I felt utterly alone, stuck at the bottom of a dark pit with no way out.

I couldn't contain the rage and confusion that spiraled inside me. In a blind fit of fury, I smashed the window of my '54 Chevy. I drove Jeannie home and dropped her off, my heart a wreck, before blindly heading back to my own empty house. I stumbled into the kitchen, went straight to the medicine cabinet, and grabbed two new bottles of aspirin. Without a second thought, I swallowed both bottles—200 pills, I didn't know if that was enough. It felt like the only way out of the crushing emotional weight I was carrying. The pain was unbearable, so deep and sharp that I needed it to stop. I just wanted everything to turn off, once and for all.

The pit of depression was deep and dark. It felt like the blackness was all-encompassing, and I was utterly alone in the universe. It wasn't just Jeannie—it was the overwhelming sense of hopelessness and the feeling that I didn't belong anywhere, a weight that had been with me as long as I could remember. A deep fear of rejection that haunted every part of me.

That night, I went to bed fully expecting not to wake up. I remember lying there, feeling like I was slipping in and out of consciousness, floating between life and death. It was a strange sensation, like my spirit was quietly slipping away. My parents, my brother, and my sister were all asleep, completely unaware of the crisis unfolding just a few feet away.

Around midnight, I woke to frantic banging at my window.

Even though I was barely conscious, I managed to force myself up and look out the window. There she was—Jeannie. She was banging and calling my name, trying to get me to wake up. She had walked over a mile, in the dark, from her house to mine, wearing only her pajamas and housecoat.

Something—or Someone—had awakened her in the middle of the night, and she knew she had to get to me. She had no idea what was happening, but she knew it was an emergency. She didn't even bother to get dressed—she moved so quickly. The hidden world, the same invisible friend who had shown up before in moments like the surfing accident, had invaded my life once again —speaking clearly to Jeannie, urging her with an undeniable sense of urgency. Nothing would stop her from getting to me. Through Jeannie, my cosmic, invisible friend had saved my life once again.

She grabbed the keys to my '54 Chevy and rushed me to the hospital—in pajamas and house slippers. I was in excruciating pain, drifting in and out of consciousness. I have no idea how she managed to get me into the car.

Her presence, in those moments, was more than just a physical act of saving me—it was as if the universe itself had aligned to make sure I had one last chance. I'd been drowning in self-doubt and pain for so long, but in that moment, I wasn't alone. I don't think Jeannie even realized how much her simple act of coming for me would affect the course of my life. She didn't just save my body that night—she gave me a glimpse of something greater, something that would eventually lead me to understand that I wasn't alone in my suffering. Maybe I didn't know it at the time, but in her desperation to get to me, I began to see a glimmer of hope.

At the hospital, the doctor didn't believe me. He made me vomit, then sent me home like it was nothing. In those days, teenagers didn't try to kill themselves—at least not out loud—so he dismissed me. Jeannie drove me back to her parents' house, and by the next morning, I was collapsing again. This time, the bleeding was real and impossible to ignore. My eyes were bloodshot pools, my stomach tearing itself apart. I was rushed back to the hospital, and only then did they realize I had swallowed enough aspirin to kill me—several times over.

My parents were completely shocked when they found out what had happened. They had no idea any of this was going on. Jeannie's parents arrived early in the morning, bringing me home. The chaos—the banging on the window, me stumbling out of the house and being driven to the hospital—hadn't woken them at all.

My mom and stepdad came to the hospital to visit. Bill, usually so stoic and reserved, was visibly shaken. He couldn't believe I'd done this to myself. He told me he loved me, that he was sorry for not being there when I needed him most. It was unlike him to show such raw emotion, but there he was—opening up, vulnerable in a way I'd never seen before. He told me how proud he was of me, how smart I was, how much he appreciated my help with his spelling and correspondence. I felt a mix of disbelief and gratitude. The words he said, the love I could feel in them, made me weep. I felt so sick, ashamed, helpless, and alone.

Bill's words reached me in a way I didn't expect. For a moment, I felt seen—like I mattered. Like I was enough. Then my mom walked in. Her face was twisted in anger.

"How could you do this to me?" she spat.

The words hit like a slap. Shame and fury burned through me all at once. I turned to the nurse. "Please—get her the hell out of here!"

It was like being back at square one, where nothing I did was ever right, where I was just a disappointment to the one person I needed the most. It was a devastating moment.

After the suicide attempt, my mom didn't want me to come home. Honestly, I didn't really want to either. It felt like too much, too soon, too broken. That's when my Aunt Dimple stepped in. She took me in without hesitation, moving me into her home with her husband, Put, and their four kids. She treated me like one of her own. She was kind, patient, and tried to help me heal in the way she knew how. It wasn't perfect, but it was a safe place in the middle of all the chaos.

By the time senior year came around, I went back home, but things were far from peaceful. It wasn't a happy reunion, and the tension between us was as thick as ever. One day, I came home from school to find a packed bag sitting on the front porch. I asked my mom what it was for.

"You're moving," she said.

"I am?" I asked, caught off guard.

She looked at me and said, "It's you or Bill—and it's not gonna be Bill."

The parents of one of my friends agreed to let me stay with them for the rest of the school year. Living with Tom was interesting. We drove his parents crazy pulling pranks on each other—like when I swapped out his water with vinegar, and when he drank it, the scream he let out was pure gold. Of course, it wasn't long before our prank war reached ridiculous levels, and eventually, Tom's parents had enough. No hard feelings, though; I understood.

At the end of the year, I enlisted in the Air Force. Jeannie and I worked things out, and we spent the rest of high school together. We married at 19, right after I joined the Air Force.

This part of my life still brings up feelings of shame and guilt. The suicide attempt is something I kept hidden from everyone, including my friends. I was too embarrassed to talk about it. It felt like an unspeakable secret I couldn't share with anyone. Looking back, I realize now that it's impossible for anyone who hasn't been trapped in that kind of deep depression to understand why someone would feel like suicide is the only way out. It's easy to judge from the outside, but what's really needed in moments like these is compassion and love, not judgment.

Yet through it all, I became acutely aware that it wasn't Jeannie who saved my life that night. Her presence wasn't just the act of a concerned girlfriend rushing to help—there was something more to it. It was divine intervention. *Someone* was there.

In the midst of the chaos, a new awareness began to stir within me. I didn't fully understand it at the time, but it was a dramatic confirmation that I wasn't just drifting aimlessly, that there was something—or someone—watching over me. It was a feeling I'd had as a child, but this time it wasn't just a vague presence—it was real. This invisible force had shown up to save me again. Through Jeannie, the Spirit of God broke into my darkness. She wasn't just a girlfriend in pajamas pounding on my window. She was listening to something or *Someone* deep inside her—an urgency she couldn't explain.

That night marked the beginning of something I had been too afraid to acknowledge. It wasn't just the physical act of being saved; it was the dawning realization that I might have a connection to something greater, something that cared for me when I couldn't care for myself. I didn't know it yet, but this invisible Presence—my cosmic Friend—wasn't just a fleeting feeling or a near-miss.

I didn't understand it then. I only knew this: I should've been dead. Somehow, I wasn't.

I needed to know who this loving Presence was, and what He had to do with me. My search for truth would send me racing toward my own private hell—convinced it was freedom.

PART TWO
BLOWS AGAINST THE EMPIRE

"It was my own personal manifesto. A generational battle cry—the broken upside-down cross our banner, a rejection of everything I had once known. And I was ready to burn it all down."

CHAPTER SIX

BREAKING RANKS

By 1966, the Vietnam War was really heating up, and the draft was taking thousands of us into a crazy war against our wills. For many of us, it felt like the world was coming apart. At 19, I enlisted in the Air Force to avoid the draft with the intention of marrying Jeannie after my training was completed. It wasn't out of patriotism or even ambition—it was survival. The Army and the Marines were sending boys my age to Vietnam, and too many of them weren't coming back. I figured the Air Force was my best chance to stay alive. But almost immediately, I knew I didn't fit. Military life wasn't the place for someone like me.

Jeannie and I married after I finished basic training. We had a huge Catholic wedding in our hometown and then moved to my first duty station in Spokane, Washington.

After basic training, I went through medical training in Montgomery, Alabama—deep in the segregated South. I had never seen anything like it. Whites-only signs were still posted on restrooms and drinking fountains. Separate schools, whites-only

toilets and drinking fountains, and even separate ambulances. I
was shocked to see ambulances with blue lights for blacks and red
lights for whites. The Civil Rights Act of 1964 and the Voting
Rights Act of 1965 had passed, but you wouldn't have known it
from walking down the streets of Montgomery. The hostility was
still thick in the air, and the "separate but equal" lie was alive and
well.

For a kid from California, where we didn't know of such
things, it felt like another world—one that slapped me in the face
every single day. Alabama was still clinging to segregation like it
hadn't lost the fight, and the military's blind loyalty to the war
effort only made it worse. I didn't fit the mold they wanted. I spoke
up too much, pushed back too hard, and I earned a reputation as a
troublemaker—a peacenik.

My views didn't sit well with the brass. They wanted
obedience; I gave them questions. They wanted blind loyalty, but I
gave them protest. The clash finally came to a head when, in a
moment of raw frustration with a system that felt oppressive and
unjust, I assaulted a Bird Colonel. That single act could have
landed me in Leavenworth. Instead, to avoid embarrassment to the
Air Force, they shipped me as far away as they could. Sending me
to a tiny base in southern Japan.

I spent nearly two years in Japan as a medical/dental
specialist. Off base, I rented an upstairs room from the Nishihara
family, who lived in a centuries-old house built without nails, only
hand-hewn joinery—a quiet emblem of the peace I was chasing.
My rent was providing English lessons for their two children.

Their home sat beside a Shinto-Buddhist monastery. From my
window, I watched monks in saffron robes quietly move through
their rituals. How had they found peace while I wrestled to taste

it? Their religion fascinated me. It was so foreign to my Judeo-Christian view of a God above creation.

Their lives, ordered by ritual, seemed to lift them above the chaos. I didn't know the sutras they chanted or the gods they prayed to, but I envied their calm. Sometimes I wondered if they had found the secret to life that always eluded me. Watching them, I felt both restless and strangely hopeful—as if maybe peace wasn't a lie after all.

While I was in Japan, Jeannie gave birth to our first child, Annie. She was no accident; we carefully planned for the pregnancy before I left the country. I wasn't there for her arrival, but I tried to be as present as I could from across the ocean. I wrote to her almost daily while she was still in the womb—letters full of hopes, dreams, and the love of a young father aching to meet his daughter. Jeannie kept all these letters. Decades later, before she passed away, Jeannie gave those letters to Annie. She told me she wept as she read them, realizing how deeply I had loved her even before she was born. Looking back, that meant everything—being apart from her was a big hole in my heart.

When Annie finally arrived, I was granted immediate leave. I flew home to California, held her in my arms, and gave her the name Michelle Ann Marie—after our mothers. Leaving her behind at the end of that month was one of the hardest things I had ever done. I carried her face with me back to Japan, tucked alongside the Buddhist sutras I was reading. For all my talk of peace, nothing pierced me more than the ache of being separated from her.

That curiosity pulled me deeper. I began reading Buddhist philosophy, drawn to its message of peace and its rejection of violence. For the first time, I saw the possibility of a different kind of existence from my Western mindset. I wandered temples and forests, soaking in a way of life that felt ancient and unhurried. With Jeannie back in the States, I could throw myself even more deeply into the search for peace.

In Beppu, I entered the cavernous belly of the largest Buddha in Japan, built with the ashes of 50,000 people. The statue rose 85 feet, and inside, tunnels wound deep into the earth. Hundreds of small Buddhas, each with a red apron, lined the walls. Candles flickered in the thick, still air—mystery pressing close. It was the opposite of the chaos I had left behind.

My curiosity grew into conviction. I embraced the Buddhist call to nonviolence—*do no harm*. Their promise of peace and the end of suffering sounded like the truth I'd been searching for. I wandered temples and forests, telling myself I was finding answers, but the deeper I went, the less certain I became. Was I discovering truth, or just stumbling down someone else's road? Buddha himself had been a Hindu who walked away, still searching. And truth is—I didn't know what in the hell I was doing.

Japan planted a seed in me. The rituals, the philosophy of nonviolence, the promise of peace—I carried all of it back to California. And when I returned, I found an entire generation searching for the same thing, though in very different ways.

Back in the Bay Area, I landed right in the middle of a cultural revolution. Berkeley was boiling over—students taking over buildings, shouting down their professors, demanding freedom to say and do whatever they wanted. The women's movement was shaking the old order too—bras tossed in trash cans, beauty contests mocked, rules of appearance ridiculed. I saw it with my own eyes and knew the world my parents' generation lived in was gone.

At the same time, my friends talked endlessly about communes and a new way of living—everyone sharing everything, no rules, no limits. It sounded beautiful, but even then, I wondered, *how do you build a world on nothing but slogans and rebellion?* We thought we were escaping selfishness, but in truth, we were just dressing it up in new clothes.

In hindsight, it is easy to see these things. But when you are caught up in the moment—the excitement, the drama of some new thing, a different way of seeing—it is a powerful agent of *delusion.*

I didn't know it then, but this would morph into what we now call the New Age Movement—a wave that would deeply influence my generation and change the course of history.

As the movement spread, so did the countercultural ideals, and I, along with millions of others, was swept up in it all—intoxicated by the idea of unbridled individual freedom. I believed we could leave the old world behind, create a new one—but how could we, when the movement was rooted in the very same self-centeredness it was trying to escape? In the long run, this throwing off of all morality and basic responsibility, to pursue personal pleasure, was the very thing that destroyed the movement. I thought about these things, but plunged forward, disregarding the warnings right in front of me.

Like my hippie friends, I was blind to this and kept pursuing the ideal that truth is whatever you choose to believe. Along with millions of baby boomers, I was intoxicated or drunk on the idea of unbridled individual freedom, even while pushing the concept of communes. How would that ever work? In retrospect, it seems oxymoronic. We thought we were entering into a new, natural lifestyle of brotherhood and peace, just hoping it would all work out.

The sexual revolution didn't stop at communes. The gay scene exploded, and many of my friends in San Francisco were experimenting with relationships that would've been unthinkable only a decade earlier. I didn't judge—I wanted to belong to this "society" of free thinkers, and who was I to draw the line? We all wanted the same thing—to be free of labels, free of rules, free of the weight of anyone telling us how to live. But freedom without any anchor wasn't really freedom at all.

And the war was always there, in the background, pressing on everything. Vietnam wasn't just headlines—it was boys my age, shipped out and chewed up. I was out of the military and joined as a protester when the tension exploded at Fort Ord. The Lesbian Coalition and Gay Liberation Front called a massive anti-war protest outside the base. The war in Vietnam was raging, and thousands of young men were being sent off to fight in a conflict that many of us couldn't understand—and we vehemently opposed.

We stood outside the gates, shouting, "STOP THE WAR! PEACE NOW!" Our voices rose together as the soldiers stood at attention, rifles in hand, staring past us. Some of the marchers pushed flowers into the barrels of their guns, as if peace could be forced into existence. It looked beautiful and foolish all at once.

For a moment, it felt like history itself was trembling. I was right in the middle of it, swept up in the noise, the fists raised, the belief that we could change the world. But deep down, something felt off.

We said love. What we meant was freedom from responsibility.

We said peace. What we meant was rebellion.

We said revolution. What we meant was escape.

The remnants of my Sunday school teaching were still whispering that this wasn't going to end the way we hoped. We promised a new world, but we were building it on sand. If the protests couldn't deliver peace, maybe something else could.

CHAPTER SEVEN
ILLUSIONS IN THE BALANCE

I got swept up in the words of Timothy Leary, the pied piper of psychedelics, and Richard Alpert, his Harvard partner, who later became Baba Ram Dass. Leary preached LSD like it was a ticket to the cosmos, while Alpert turned from chemicals to yoga, meditation, and Eastern mysticism. His book *Be Here Now* became scripture for a whole generation. I wasn't just reading their ideas—I was living them.

A core tenet of this new philosophy was the concept of the Great Spirit or life force—a Native American idea of God—along with the belief in the deification of the earth. This idea drew from different traditions and was often referred to in New Age circles as Gaia, or Mother of Creation. I called it the "cosmic glue" philosophy, a belief that everything was interconnected. I resonated with it, convinced there was more to this world than the material. I knew it, not just as an idea, but from experience. Something unseen had always been at work around me, and I was desperate to understand it. But the more I explored, the more I realized that this belief stood in contrast to my earlier experiences of a very personal, loving God.

By 1967, their message had caught fire. "Turn on, tune in, drop out" became the mantra of a movement, especially during California's "Summer of Love" in Golden Gate Park. LSD, marijuana, mescaline, and peyote were treated like sacraments to a generation desperate for meaning.

Aldous Huxley's *The Doors of Perception*, about his mescaline experience, deeply influenced me and sparked my curiosity about mind-expanding drugs. I dove headfirst into them—taking massive doses that hurled me into realms I couldn't have imagined. Each trip cracked open my world—unity in creation, glimpses of dimensions beyond sight or sound. The experiences only deepened my hunger to find the truth behind it all. But then I saw the flaw—every "vision" came from swallowing a pill or chewing a cactus.

If I needed chemicals to touch the invisible, how real could it be?

The movement was massive, with young people flocking to San Francisco, drawn by the promises of the New Age and the anthem, *If You're Going to San Francisco*. The Haight-Ashbury district became a mecca for hippies, who believed they were returning to a simpler, more peaceful time. As corny as it seemed, the song became an anthem, and the hippies were dubbed "flower children." Soon, San Francisco and the Haight-Ashbury neighborhood were teeming with tens of thousands, all hoping the New Age of Aquarius was real—that we were returning to the garden. But the truth was far from what we had imagined. It was all an illusion. The reality was ugly. What I thought was the edge of something beautiful turned out to be the complete opposite.

The disillusionment hit harder than I had expected, a harsh awakening to the truth that our dreams were just that—dreams.

Meanwhile, the Woodstock Music Festival on August 15, 1969, drew hundreds of thousands to Max's 600-acre farm in upstate New York. It was hailed as a symbol of harmony, a place where people could live together in peace, even in the pouring rain. Though the festival was marked by drug use, the hippies seemed to care for one another, and there was little violence, despite the crowd of over 400,000. For all its excess, Woodstock carried a strange sense of care—even in the mud and rain, people shared food, blankets, whatever they had. It felt like a glimpse of what we longed for. But back in San Francisco, the dream was already rotting.

By 1969, the experiment in San Francisco had turned into a nightmare. When I walked Haight-Ashbury, once the symbol of the "Age of Aquarius," it wasn't the dream we'd been promised. The streets reeked of garbage and vomit, kids high on heroin and cocaine slumped against buildings, predators circling like vultures. The "Age of Aquarius" looked more like a graveyard of broken teenagers. I'd come hoping for peace and love, but what I saw was chaos. And still—I kept searching, convinced there had to be something more.

I had become a committed vegetarian, so strict that I wouldn't eat anything with a face: no meat, no fish, not even eggs. Killing sentient beings, I believed, meant more reincarnations, more suffering. As I progressed in my disciplines, I later practiced celibacy and tried to strip myself of every passion and desire, convinced that purity of thought and deed would bring enlightenment. I even refused to kill a mosquito.

At the same time, I devoured every spiritual book I could find

—Mexican shamanism, the Egyptian and Tibetan Books of the Dead, Hindu texts like the Bhagavad-Gita, the Vedas, the Upanishads. Page after page, I searched for the hidden thread that tied it all together. I called it the "cosmic glue." But no matter how far I read, the god I met there was impersonal—nothing like the invisible Friend I'd known as a boy.

That contradiction haunted me. The philosophies promised peace through oneness with the Atman or cosmic force, but my invisible Friend had been personal. He had a voice, even if I didn't yet know His name. The Eastern gods felt distant. My invisible Friend never was. I could hear His voice clearly and closely inside of me and all around me.

And still, Jesus was the last place I would look.

CHAPTER EIGHT
ALTAMONT CHAOS

By late summer 1969, I received an early discharge from the Air Force, allowing me to start college that September. I enrolled at a local community college, carrying a heavy course load. My plan at the time was to push through and make it into dental school. I did well in the subjects that interested me and not so well in the ones that bored me. My days started early—7:00 a.m. classes, five days a week. To get to my first class, I'd climb a wide set of steps that led up to the main entrance of the school.

Most mornings, as I climbed those steps, I'd pass a bearded, long-haired, barefoot hippie. He stood there in ragged clothes with a Bible raised in his hand, calling out to anyone who walked by that we needed to repent and give our lives to Jesus. I didn't understand why he unsettled me so much. My mom and dad weren't religious, but when I stayed with my grandmother and cousins on weekends, I'd sometimes go with them to the Church of Christ. In Sunday school, I'd heard the old stories about Moses,

Abraham, and Noah, and I'd heard about Jesus too—but as a kid, I never really got it.

What he was preaching from that Bible was the opposite of the path I was on, but I couldn't seem to get the picture of him—barefoot, waving that Bible, calling people to repent—out of my head.

It wasn't all bad when I returned home from my military service in Japan. Jeannie had found a great apartment—cozy, with a fireplace, conveniently close to her work, and not far from the shores of San Francisco Bay. I found work nights at a local bar and pizza parlor—making pizzas and sometimes breaking up fights as a bouncer. Most evenings, I'd head straight there after class around 6:00 p.m., work until closing at 2:00 a.m., then catch a few hours of sleep before my 7:00 a.m. classes. It was a grind—never enough sleep, homework piling up, and weekends spent just trying to catch up.

Because my schedule was so crazy, I didn't get to spend as much time with Annie as I wanted, but Jeannie and I took whatever time was available to do things with her. Being with her was such a joy, and watching her grow was miraculous. She was just a little over a year old by this time, and being with her was the best time of my life. When I was at school and Jeannie was at work, my mom, who doted on Annie, would care for her at her home.

I even had an inside track to Georgetown Dental School—a doctor I'd worked for in the Air Force had an uncle who was dean of admissions and said he'd help me if I finished my prerequisites. But college felt so middle-class and irrelevant. Hundreds of thousands of us were rejecting what society expected. I didn't want the middle-class path. I wanted out. It was a massive counterculture rebellion. So I decided to pursue the counterculture, New Age lifestyle.

After I dropped out, I spent most days watching Annie—those months became some of my sweetest memories. Even though I dropped out of school, I still had to pay bills. At night, I still worked at the pizza parlor, but that would soon come to an end.

While I was at Mr. F's pizza parlor, something happened that began to crack my belief in the "peace and love" ideals the hippie movement was touting. I'd missed out on the "Three Days of Peace and Music" at Woodstock in August 1969, where around 400,000 people gathered to hear their favorite bands and, supposedly, help create a new social order. But I wasn't going to miss out again. In December of that year, another opportunity for me to experience this so-called "unified spirit" came around. A rock concert was being organized at Altamont Speedway in the East Bay hills, just outside San Francisco. The Rolling Stones, The Grateful Dead, and most of the San Francisco rock bands were slated to perform.

Determined not to miss this West Coast version of Woodstock, I went to my boss and asked for the night off. It was December 6th, 1969—Saturday night—and our pizza place would be packed. It was one of the busiest nights of the year. My boss told me I couldn't have the night off. I wasn't having it. I was committed to seeing this peace and love gathering with my own eyes, so I told him I quit. That's right—I quit. The thought of experiencing it all in person—the music, the crowd, the culture—made me feel like I was stepping into something historic. I could hardly contain my excitement.

Jeannie was equally thrilled. We were about to be part of history—our generation's history. We'd be there, surrounded by like-minded people, listening to the Rolling Stones, Jefferson Airplane, and all the bands that defined our time.

Late in the afternoon, Jeannie and I hopped onto my road racing motorcycle and headed to the concert. We were both excited. The ride felt like freedom—the kind only a bike can give. Roaring down the 580 freeway at 75 miles an hour, we felt the wind in our faces when suddenly, an even louder, deafening roar surged up behind us.

I turned my head in shock to see a swarm of dozens of Harley Davidson motorcycles closing in at high speed. We were soon engulfed in a massive group of riders—Hell's Angels, unmistakable, in their colors: a skull with wings and "Hells Angels" emblazoned above the death's head on the back of their jackets. It was an intimidating sight.

For Jeannie and me, it was terrifying. We were on a Japanese bike, and the Angels clearly had no intention of letting us out of their circle. They didn't let us escape. Surrounded by the roar of Harleys, we felt small, vulnerable—trapped in their midst.

We rode with them for about twenty minutes, as they led us off the freeway and onto the road that led to the Speedway, still tightly packed in the middle of their intimidating circle.

I was familiar with Hell's Angels, having grown up in the Bay Area. When I was 11 or 12, I had neighbors who were Angels. One of them used to give me rides on the back of his Harley, and at the time, I thought it was hot stuff riding around my neighborhood with an Angel. But years later, I realized they weren't the romanticized figures I had once seen them as. They were just thugs—and I knew firsthand what they were capable of.

They had murdered a childhood friend of mine over a drug deal gone bad. They shot him and then burned him alive in his car.

That memory hit me like a hammer as I realized just how dangerous the situation was. My fear was not imaginary.

When we arrived at the concert, the 580 interstate freeway had turned into a parking lot. Hundreds of cars were parked and left in the driving lanes and on the shoulder of the road. It was chaos—I had never seen anything like it. The Angels parked their bikes off to the side, and we were swept along with the tide of bikers as we all made our way to the concert grounds.

The air was thick with the anticipation of a wild time, and the Angels were pumped up, rowdy, ready for whatever chaos the night might bring. Jeannie and I were trapped in the middle of these bikers and carried along with them all. We had no choice but to follow the crowd, moving with the flow.

As we got closer to the stage, we had to sit down near a group of Angels, just beneath a big school bus that had been driven onto the grounds. More than a dozen Angels had climbed to the top of the bus, and they were roaring drunk. One of them, wearing a full wolf pelt—including the wolf's head—danced and whooped, completely lost in the chaos.

The atmosphere was wild. The bikers threw full beer cans into the crowd of concertgoers below. The crowd was massive—over 400,000 people, including women and children of all ages, spread out across the vast field, completely exposed to the mayhem above.

The air was thick with tension, and it felt like the whole event was teetering on the edge. What was supposed to be a day of peace and love was quickly morphing into something unrecognizable.

Everyone came to Altamont hoping for a great time, a sense of camaraderie, and the unity promised by the West Coast version of Woodstock. But the Hell's Angels seemed intent on getting drunker and more out of control with each passing moment.

We could hear the screams as the heavy beer cans began striking people in the crowd. I could see the horrified, bewildered looks on the faces of the hippies—many of them had brought their families, hoping for a day of peace and love—and now, they were witnessing the violent chaos unfold right before their eyes.

When Jefferson Airplane, one of the most popular San Francisco bands, took the stage to start their set, the mood shifted violently. A drunken Hell's Angel jumped up onto the stage, and the band's drummer and vocalist, Marty Balin, tried to reason with him, pleading for him to get down. But the Angel violently attacked Marty, knocking him unconscious. Grace Slick, the band's lead singer, wasted no time. She jumped onto the back of the Angel, cursing and pummeling him with all her strength. The chaos blasted through the microphones, echoing across the field.

As this madness unfolded, we saw a massive helicopter landing at the edge of the field—the Rolling Stones had arrived, ready to perform. Watching them and their entourage make their way towards the stage, I couldn't shake the deep sense of fear and foreboding that had settled in my gut. Something was terribly wrong, and I had the overwhelming feeling that things were about to get much worse.

Jeannie and I sat in the middle of a large group of drunk and rowdy Hell's Angels, feeling the pressure of the tension rise around us. It was clear that the day of peace and love we had hoped for was slipping away fast. Everything felt like it was careening downhill.

So much for peace and love. Jeannie and I were devastated. We pushed our way out of the crowd and left Altamont Speedway, escaping the turmoil. We returned to our motorcycle and rode home, both of us shaken by the events we had witnessed. As we rode, I couldn't stop thinking about the foreboding I felt in my gut —it was real. I was deeply thankful we had left when we did.

Shortly after we left, all hell broke loose. Chaos erupted in the crowd, with people screaming and running for their lives. The Hell's Angels had stabbed a man to death—allegedly for pulling a gun on them. This happened just below where we had been seated, and it was the violent climax to a day that had promised so much but delivered the complete opposite.

Hundreds of thousands had come for a dream. What they got was violence, fear, and disillusionment.

I was done. There had to be something better, something real. Doubts were growing in my mind about the direction I was going. Was this "turn on, tune in, drop out" philosophy really going to work out, or was I just chasing a pipe dream? Was it possible for people to really change? I was already in deep.

Footnote: Incredibly, the Angels had actually been hired as "security"—paid with 300 cases of beer. Looking back, it seems unbelievable that anyone thought that would end well.

In the aftermath, people said Altamont marked the death of the hippie dream. For me, it tore the mask off. Peace and love had been a lie, and I couldn't unsee it.

CHAPTER NINE

WHEN THE EARTH SPOKE

Some of our best times as a family came in the wild places. Jeannie, little Annie, and I would head north with old high school friends—many of whom had slipped fully into hippie life—and spend days deep in the Salmon-Trinity Wilderness of Northern California—backpacking, camping by rivers, cooking over campfires. Smoking pot and trying psychedelics were just part of the scene. Sometimes there were twenty of us—mostly couples and kids—camped along an isolated Humboldt County river, like one big family. Annie toddled barefoot in the sand with the dogs, and every now and then, an occasional hiker would stumble onto our camp of naked hippies and look pretty shocked.

We'd catch salmon and trout, roast them over the fire, and stay for a week or more—eating, laughing, and enjoying old friendships. When we weren't in the mountains, Jeannie and I loved the coast with our two dogs—Sloopy and Zombie. Weekends were for camping and hiking the beaches of Marin, Mendocino, and Humboldt—walking the dunes barefoot, picking up shells and pieces of sea glass, swimming in the cold waves, and exploring the sea caves at low tide while our dogs ran up and down the beach. Those were good times for the three of us. Sadly, they didn't last.

Our home life was getting more strained as I went deeper into Eastern religion and the world of psychedelics and mystical experience. Jeannie and I were drifting further apart. We weren't getting along and argued a lot. She wasn't willing to take the plunge into a totally different reality and culture from the one we had both been raised in. I wanted her to see what I was seeing, but it was impossible for her.

Jeannie was a Roman Catholic and believed in its teachings, while I was raised in a non-religious home. My exposure to Christianity was through my grandmother, aunts, and cousins, who I had said before were committed to the fundamentalist Church of Christ.

By then, I had almost become a stranger to Jeannie. She was just so level-headed and practical, while I had become a mystic and a dreamer. She couldn't understand what it was that I was searching for. She was happy just to be a wife and a mother and didn't understand why that wasn't enough for me.

However, hindsight is perfect... time has proven that Jeannie was right.

Our paths split completely when I decided to throw myself into the New Age culture and the search for virtue, non-violence, and the purification and transformation of mankind—the Eastern path of dharma. Jeannie just wanted a normal life centered on family and home. She was a wonderful, giving person, but my choices and dreams weren't hers.

I wanted something more. I was looking for what was behind the curtain of this material existence. I knew something was there.

I had to find it—that invisible dimension I had sensed as a kid. I was taking psychedelic trips on peyote, mescaline, and LSD, and believed, at the time, those were authentic spiritual experiences.

One experience in particular set the scene for my deep dive into Eastern mysticism. I enthusiastically accepted the belief that the earth itself was alive. And everything on it was divine, sacred, worthy of reverence. In Greek mysticism, the Earth was considered the mother of creation and was referred to as Gaia. In New Age consciousness teaching, this became an important aspect of returning to nature and doing no harm to the Earth.

I became more and more radical in my belief that humans were destroying the Earth. I believed they were raping Mother Earth by mining, damming rivers, logging forests, and drilling for oil. I got so lost in it, I even thought it'd be okay for millions to live without clean water or electricity if it 'saved' the planet. I found out as I continued down this path that I was tragically mistaken.

Seismic faults were forming in my cosmic-glue religion. Something mystical was happening to me, and I needed to know by whom—or what.

In the hip culture of the Bay Area, Mount Tamalpais in Marin County was believed to be a place of great spiritual energy. Other peaks—Mount Diablo, Mount Shasta, Mount Lassen—were seen as cosmic vortexes. Native people had long regarded them as sacred.

At the time, I had a friend in Berkeley who was synthesizing pharmaceutical LSD in one of the university labs. We believed these substances opened doors to higher consciousness. Eastern mysticism spoke of such realms, accessed through meditation, fasting, and yoga. LSD, to us, was a shortcut—a direct line to those transcendent states. It was pure, potent, and unlike anything you'd find on the street.

One weekend a few of us set out early for the Mt. Tamalpais summit, knowing it was going to be a long hike. At the trailhead, we sat down and took an exceptionally large dose of LSD. The typical dose was around 225 micrograms and lasted eight hours. We took many times that amount, preparing ourselves for a journey that would stretch our consciousness beyond imagination.

About an hour in, the acid kicked in. As I climbed the trail, everything changed. I noticed the tiniest details— a small blue flower that might have once gone unnoticed now glowed with divine beauty. The rustling wind through the trees sounded like water. Everything was heightened.

The world around me came alive. Colors radiated with energy, vibrating with a life I had never noticed before. The trees shimmered as if electric, their aura alive. Nature wasn't just surrounding me—it was me. I wasn't looking at beauty; I was *part* of it.

I had always sensed there was more to life than what I could touch and see. Now, I was immersed in it. What once seemed ordinary—the stone beneath my feet, the leaf fluttering in the wind, the ant marching across the trail—now appeared profoundly beautiful.

Always in the back of my mind was the question, *Who is responsible for the wonder of this creation? And why is it here?*

My sense of unity deepened. I couldn't separate myself from the forest or the sky. I had become one with creation. From the tiniest atom to the vast expanse of the universe, every part of creation radiated meaning and purpose—anchored in the awareness that it all existed in the mind of some greater being.

I didn't have words for it then, but there was always a sense that the beauty pointed beyond itself—like Someone was behind it, even if I didn't know who.

I came upon a massive set of boulders and climbed up. They stood like ancient elephants basking in the sun. I stretched out on the warm stone, soaking in the light, and that's when it happened —a mystical experience that still echoes in me today.

Lying on that rock, I felt deeply connected to the earth. I saw through the eyes of the stone—timeless, ancient. I sensed the power and wisdom of the planet. It was as if I'd pressed my ear to the heartbeat of the universe, and it was whispering secrets I couldn't yet translate.

This was more than a psychedelic trip. It was the beginning of my search for the One who created all of it.

I could see Mt. Diablo standing as a lonely sentinel high above the hills of the East Bay. For thousands of years, I have looked from this mountain top and seen the beautiful dance and symphony of a creation that is vibrating with life. I am one with this life. It is me and all mankind, and it has been given to us by someone, some great Spirit, and He has given us the eyes to behold it all and is speaking to us constantly, in a whisper or a raging torrent of awareness that He exists. I must find Him. I must know Him. I cannot stop searching until I do.

This was my personal experience. I'm not saying everyone should seek transcendence through psychedelics. Years later, I came to understand that the awareness and beauty I tasted that day are accessible in even greater ways—without drugs. To me, that is God's mercy. He will use anything to reveal Himself. All He needs is a willing heart and a hunger for truth.

That said, I must also offer a warning.

One of the men who joined us that day was a childhood friend. We'd done many of these trips together. But this one broke him. He took LSD, stripped naked, and wandered into a small Bay Area town. Believing himself to be Adam, the father of humanity, he approached a woman and told her that God had called him to repopulate the earth. She screamed. Neighbors called the sheriff. He was arrested and placed on psychiatric watch. Thankfully, he recovered—and to my knowledge, never touched psychedelics again.

God used LSD in my life—but that was *my* story, not a prescription.

After that day on Mount Tamalpais, I knew I would never experience a higher spiritual revelation through drugs. I became determined to search out the truth about who created all this beauty—who held it all together and yet loved me personally.

I didn't realize I was the one who was lost—that I would not find Him. He would find me in my darkness.

CHAPTER TEN
OIL, OUTRAGE, AND THE PATH TO ISOLATION

A few days after my transcendental experience on the trail high up on Mt Tamalpais, something happened that would change the trajectory of my life forever.

I've said before—I'd become an ecofanatic. (Yes, I made that word up.) Everything was about the environment—caring for the earth, the sea, the air, the forests. I despised anything that I felt would cause harm to the natural world. My circle of friends and I were so extreme we even hatched a plan to blow up the giant steel towers that carried power lines across our favorite wildlands reserve. We were dead serious. Thank God we were interrupted before we could follow through. Otherwise, this might be a prison memoir.

Then came January 18, 1971.

Two oil tankers—the Arizona Standard and the Oregon Standard—collided beneath the Golden Gate Bridge, spilling over 800,000 gallons of fuel oil into San Francisco Bay. Headlines said it was the worst oil spill in California history; some reports said nearly a million gallons.

The devastation to the bay was beyond belief.

The entire coastline was coated in thick oil. Every gull, pelican, loon, grebe, duck, seal, and sea otter—so many species I'd loved since childhood—drenched and dying. The Audubon Society said tens of thousands of birds and mammals perished. Out of the chaos, International Bird Rescue was born, thanks in part to "long-haired hippies" who showed up by the hundreds with straw to soak up oil and save what wildlife they could.

Just days earlier, from the ancient stones of Mount Tamalpais, I'd looked out over a living, vibrant bay. Now that same view was smothered in black oil—its beauty choked under a slick of poison and death.

This tragedy struck me deeply and personally. I'd been raised on the San Francisco Bay. Some of my earliest memories are tied to that water.

The bay wasn't just part of the landscape for me—it was part of who I was. My grandfather, a ship's captain, would lift me into the wheelhouse of his giant paddlewheel ferry. The wheel towered over me, but with my little hands gripping it, I was sure I was steering us across the water. Those ferries, some dating back to the late 1800s, still sit wrecked around the shoreline—rotting, or turned into restaurants. To me, they were alive with mystery, and in my grandfather's stories, I felt the salt of generations. His own father had been shanghaied off the Barbary Coast during the Gold Rush, taken captive for seven years as a seaman. The bay ran deep in our blood.

With my stepdad, the bay wasn't just stories anymore—it was spray in my face and fish in the boat. We'd motor out to Red Rock

Island in his little fishing boat, the two of us bouncing hard over wind-whipped waves. I'd crawl under the bow to escape the icy spray, only to smack my head on the roof as the boat slammed down again. It was terrifying, and I loved every minute of it. We'd haul home coolers packed with rock cod, and I felt like a conqueror.

When I wasn't on the water, I was reading about it. I devoured Jack London's *Tales of the Fish Patrol,* picturing myself as a teenage oyster pirate in a sloop called the *Razzle Dazzle,* sneaking out at night to raid traps under the nose of the law. The bay wasn't just scenery—it was adventure, danger, and magic.

That sense of wonder was magnified at Aunt Millie's husband, Dan McCampbell's, parents' house, where the tide slapped against the foundation of their house. Their backyard was a boy's paradise—less yard, more naval scrapyard. A full submarine conning tower stood there, numbers still painted on the side, along with rusting bows of old ships, anchors big as cars, and relics from the war. I'd climb inside that conning tower, peer through the periscope, and declare myself on an "important mission" for the U.S. Navy. In my imagination, I practically won World War II from that backyard.

Of course, not all my adventures were glorious. One weekend I caught a coffee can full of mud crabs and smuggled them home, stashing the can in my bedroom closet. Life got busy, and I forgot about them. A week later, the house reeked. When my stepdad and I opened the closet, we found a can of liquefied crab sludge so foul it nearly knocked us over. He was so stunned, he forgot to give me the licking I deserved. My rear end let out a sigh of relief that matched my own.

By seventh or eighth grade, I was roaming farther—riding my

bike six miles to the shoreline near Hercules, where a dynamite plant loomed over the little company town. That factory had a deadly history—fifty-nine people killed in explosions from the late 1800s through the early 1900s. Maybe that danger is what drew me and my buddies in. On weekends when the plant was quiet, we'd sneak inside and climb into the ore carts used to haul sulfur from the ships at the dock. We'd pile in with our fishing poles, give the cart a shove, and go rumbling down the rails all the way to the end of the dock. Somehow, we never got caught. And somehow, we always caught fish.

For me, the bay was more than a backdrop. It was a living companion—mystery, danger, beauty, and joy rolled into one. Its tides carried my childhood, and its waters shaped me in ways I wouldn't understand until much later.

Looking out across San Francisco Bay—with Alcatraz and Angel Island in view, the coastal mountains framing the horizon—it was hard not to see the hand of a Creator. One verse from Sunday school always stayed with me: "God looked at all He had made, and it was good." Deep in my heart, I believed that was true. I still do.

The same waters where I once played Navy in an old conning tower were now a graveyard for birds and sea life. That broke something in me, and I'd had enough. If the world was this broken, I wanted out. I needed to find a way to live differently— somewhere far from the madness of modern society.

CHAPTER ELEVEN

THE ULTIMATUM THAT CHANGED EVERYTHING

Jeannie worked at a bank and then at a medical clinic. She wasn't into the New Age counterculture stuff, especially not the drugs. We were living in the same house but heading in different directions.

As I said before, my college career pretty much fell apart. I lost interest in school, dropped out, and dove into Eastern philosophy, shamanism, and LSD. When I left school, the G.I. Bill money stopped. I continued my night job at the pizza parlor, so for a while we lived mostly on Jeannie's income. She was a genius with finances and somehow made it work, while I stayed home with Annie during the day. I loved that time with her—she was not quite two, blonde hair, blue eyes, just a beautiful little girl.

Those months caring for her are some of my best memories. We'd lie on the floor coloring, or I'd read her stories. We'd go for walks with our dog Snoopy or hop in the car to visit friends. She was a joy, and I was sad when it ended.

After a few months, I got a job at University Laboratories in

Berkeley making helium-neon laser beams for industry. It was a good job, and my mom started watching Annie during the day.

But by then, I was going deeper and deeper into the radical stuff. By the middle of 1970, our marriage was over. I felt I was on some kind of spiritual search—still chasing the "turn on, tune in, drop out" life.

That's when Jeannie gave me an ultimatum—get it together or move out. I didn't realize then that it came from love and desperation; she wanted me present for her and Annie, not lost chasing illusions. Leaving Annie was the hardest thing I had ever done. Looking back now, I can see Jeannie was right. There was nothing more spiritual or valuable than my family. But at the time, I didn't see it. I was too committed to discovering the "truth of everything," blind to what I already had. Sometimes, finding out too late, the truth we hide from ourselves is an unexpected and bitter pill to swallow.

In the last few months of 1970, Jeannie and I were no longer living together. Our separation was tearful and painful, but she couldn't reconcile staying together when our paths had split so completely. We'd said our marriage vows in a Catholic ceremony, and I think that weighed on her. Divorce was hard for her to face. Catholic teaching said it was a mortal sin—a fast ticket to hell. But by this point, she knew it was a very real possibility.

Not living with Annie was heart-wrenching. I tried to spend as much time as I could with her, but it was difficult. Jeannie tried to facilitate my getting Annie as much as possible, but it was never enough. Jeannie always realized how important it was that I remain in Annie's life as much as possible.

As I look back on those years, the "turn on, tune in, drop out" philosophy had completely flipped the Judeo-Christian idea of morality on its head. The view of marriage and monogamy I'd grown up with was tossed aside in this new community. It had become normal in the counterculture to have multiple partners, live together until you got bored, had a falling out, or found someone you liked better.

Commitment? Covenant? Working through problems? None of that fit with the "if it feels good, do it" mindset. The song *Love the One You're With* by Crosby, Stills & Nash basically gave everyone permission to walk away from relationships for the most childish, selfish reasons.

This wasn't just some weird cult—it was a worldwide movement among college-age youth reshaping Western culture. Later, friends in Scandinavia, Europe, and Great Britain told me the same thing was happening there too.

The rock music of the time told the story. John Lennon, a new age icon from Liverpool and a founding member of the Beatles, became wildly popular along with his girlfriend, Yoko Ono. Lennon had left his first wife and son, Julian, to be with Yoko. I remember reading an interview where Julian spoke about the bitterness and pain he and his mom had experienced after the abandonment.

When I read about Julian Lennon's pain after his dad left his mom for Yoko, I felt pain in my heart that I was doing the same thing to my daughter and that I had no idea how my separation from her mom would ultimately affect her life. My natural father had abandoned my mom and me when I was just an infant. I know the repercussions were painful, long-lasting, and deep. I have no idea what his reasons were for abandonment, *but were mine any better? Would it be possible for Jeannie, Annie, and me to escape the consequences of my decisions?*

One thing that I have found out so many years after the events of my story is that there is no escape from consequences. There is nowhere to hide the pain.

In 1971, John and Yoko released an album, and the song *Imagine* became an anthem for the new age consciousness movement. In their song, Lennon and Yoko painted a picture of a world without religion, nations, or personal possessions—a kind of global utopia where humanity lived together as one. It sounded beautiful on the surface—but the entire meaning of love was missing. We were lost in a delusion.

I was blind to the impossibility of this vision working. I chose to believe we could overcome basic human nature and create a new Garden of Eden with nothing but slogans and good intentions. Too late, I realized the hippie movement wasn't about love or peace at all—it was about narcissism—everyone seeking their own way, their own desires, their own satisfaction first and foremost. The counterculture revolution I'd thrown myself into carried the seeds of its own destruction.

Plato once wrote, *"The worst of all deceptions is self-deception."* I was plunging full-speed ahead into my own cosmic version of Toad's Wild Ride. Like Toad in *The Wind in the Willows,* I was careening toward my own personal version of hell.

I really don't know why I didn't see it when it was staring me right in the face. But I didn't hear that still small voice inside—the one that had guided and protected me my whole life. Or maybe I didn't want to hear it.

In my mind, the only way forward was escape. Leave it all behind—Jeannie, Annie, middle-class America—and chase truth, whatever the cost.

The 1960s had promised a revolution of love and peace, but

what it gave me was loss, loneliness, and disillusionment. Still, I couldn't stop searching. If truth was out there, I was going to find it —even if it cost me everything.

I kept running from the God of my childhood, but no matter how far I went—into drugs, Eastern mysticism, or counterculture illusions—there was always a shadow at the edge of it all. A Presence I couldn't name, still whispering through the cracks of my rebellion.

PART THREE
CHASING EDEN

"I wasn't just leaving Babylon. I was chasing Eden. It might cost me everything. But even then, the Presence I couldn't name refused to let me go."

CHAPTER TWELVE
ARRIVAL IN EDEN

Leaving Jeannie and Annie behind had torn a hole in my heart, but I convinced myself Hawaii would be a new beginning—a place where I could finally live out the ideals I'd been chasing and find what I was looking for. I didn't see it then, but I was following in the footsteps of a father I never knew. History was repeating itself —and I was blind to it.

Hawaii, in my mind, was Eden—untouched, wild, alive with possibility.

So, I made my escape in January 1971. I sold everything I owned, which wasn't much. The one thing of real value was my beloved Suzuki road racing motorcycle. Letting that go was painful, but I was convinced paradise was worth it. A ticket to Hawaii was $75 one way, and I had no intention of ever returning to the Bay Area. At least, that's what I told myself. Truth is, I'd last about six months before the ache of being away from Annie would drag me back. That bond was too strong to ignore.

I didn't make the trip alone. Leah came with me—barefoot,

fearless, always chasing the next thrill. She was nineteen, vivacious, and the perfect picture of the freewheeling peace-and-love hippie. We had met at a party, drifted together through San Francisco's music scene, and before long, we were inseparable. She loved the Dead, the concerts, the psychedelic culture, though by that time, I had put psychedelics behind me. Our bond wasn't built on drugs anymore, but on a shared hunger for freedom and a readiness to run.

We landed in Honolulu on my birthday, January 25, 1971. Stepping off the plane felt like stepping into another world. The air wrapped around us like a blanket—hot, damp, and heavy. Coming straight from the fog and icy winds of San Francisco Bay, it was almost suffocating. The humidity clung to my skin, and I knew it would take time to get used to it.

But I wasn't here for Honolulu. I was here for the Big Island. I had heard about its wide, open spaces and endless forests, where a man could disappear into the jungle and live off the land. That's what I wanted—to leave the machinery of modern life behind and sink into something pure.

We caught a connecting flight that same day, and when we stepped off in Hilo, I was stunned. It was everything I had imagined and more.

The mountains rose above the bay like giants—Mauna Loa and Mauna Kea, both scraping the sky at nearly 14,000 feet. Tropical forest and jungle stretched for miles, thick and untamed. And the rainbows—brilliant arcs of color painted across the sky as if heaven itself had laid a brush to the clouds.

To me, those rainbows were a sign. Proof that I was on the dharma road, led by the cosmic consciousness I believed in. Deep down, my rational mind still wrestled with the idea of an impersonal cosmic mind—how could something so beautiful be impersonal? But I shoved the thought aside. I wasn't ready for questions that big. Not yet.

Hitchhiking out of Hilo, the world unfolded in every direction. On one side of the highway, the forest dripped with rain and birdsong. On the other side, the Pacific crashed against black cliffs, the spray leaping into the air. The island pulsed with life, and I felt certain I had found Eden.

When we reached a few miles north of town, another hippie pointed us toward a campsite tucked into the jungle. We found it scattered with bright tents and maybe two dozen dreamers from every corner of the States—long hair, wide eyes, all of us chasing some version of paradise. We wanted to get back to the garden. Crosby, Stills, Nash & Young had told us we could, and we believed them.

We weren't just chasing Eden—we were inventing it. For me, that meant more than herbs and rituals. I carried a little pouch around my neck, convinced it connected me to the unseen world. In some circles of the hippie community, I was already taking on the identity of a shaman or spiritual healer. (Of course, some of my friends who disagreed with my philosophies thought I was the anti-Christ. That's a whole other story!)

For us, Jethro Kloss's book *Back to Eden* was our gospel. We ate vegetables like sacraments, brewed tinctures and teas like medicine men. I carried herbs everywhere, convinced nature could heal it all. I was launching into a brave new world, full of hope, peace, and bliss. Or so I thought.

After getting absolutely drenched our first night camping on the Big Island, we decided to hitch to another part of the island. We'd heard about the Puna district—east of Hilo, on the windward side—so we packed up our camp and headed south.

What we didn't know was that, in 1971, hippies were not welcome in the Puna district. The local Hawaiians—the Kamaaina—wanted nothing to do with us. We were completely unaware that hippies there were being badly beaten, raped, and in some cases, disappearing altogether. A young hippie girl had recently been found raped and beaten to death in a lava cave—just before we arrived.

We followed the Kapoho-Kalapana road until we found a campground near the ocean. We were completely clueless and ended up in an area that was strictly off-limits to *haoles* (white people).

The coastline was called Opihikao. We pitched our tent in a small fishing village next to McKenzie Park—also known as Isaac Hale State Park, or Pohoiki Bay.

McKenzie Park sat high on the cliffs above the ocean, where massive swells crashed against the lava rock in thunderous white foam. The forest of ironwood trees looked almost like the pines I'd known in California, their needles softening the ground beneath our feet.

There were picnic tables set around the park. On the surface, it seemed like an ideal place for a family to relax and enjoy the beauty of Hawaii. But I'd read a little about McKenzie Park and knew it wasn't a popular spot for the local Hawaiians. They believed the ghosts of the prisoners who built the park in the 1800s still haunted the area.

The locals were highly superstitious, still practicing many

ancient Hawaiian traditions and following old folklore. Most of the time, the park was deserted. Occasionally, we'd see a few passing haole picnickers—but not often.

As we settled into our camp, we would walk a short distance to the ocean and watch the Hawaiian fishermen launch their boats at the Pohoiki boat ramp. We were amazed to see them bring in large sea turtles and all kinds of fish. These people truly lived off the sea.

For the most part, the locals ignored us—but there was definitely no aloha spirit coming our way.

Near the boat ramp stood a big white house with a wraparound porch. I noticed a group of young Hawaiian men and teenagers often sitting there, smoking weed. In Hawaii, they called it *pakalolo*—crazy weed. One guy, who seemed to be their leader, usually sat in a rocking chair.

One day, several of the boys came over to our camp. These young guys drove around in a lowered Chevy, like the low-riders you'd see among Latino groups back in California. They looked like young punks or toughs, and I was both curious and a little scared as they came up.

They asked if they could sit down. Of course, I agreed and welcomed them to the camp.

As it turned out, they were very superstitious and had been watching me. They were especially interested in the pouch I wore around my neck. The young *Kanaka* who seemed to be their leader cautiously asked me what was in the bag. His name was Keoli.

At the time, I was wearing white cotton Mexican peon clothing with bells sewn around the edges of my shirt. My beard was long and full, and my hair hung uncut to my shoulders. My clothes were embroidered with rainbows and flowers, and my feet were bare.

I was quite a curiosity to these young Hawaiians. I was probably one of the first hippies they'd met up close—without beating him to a pulp.

I carefully poured the contents of my "magic bag" onto the table. Crystals glinted in the sun, a gold nugget caught the light, and bones lay beside a petrified dinosaur gizzard, which I was sure had mystical force. The Kanakas' eyes grew wide. Then came the question, spoken in all sincerity and fear: "Bruddah John, you aren't going to witch us, are you?"

I assured them that I only used my magic for good and would never try to harm them.

As it turned out, these were the very *Kanakas* who had been attacking and terrorizing hippies in their neighborhood.

By this time, I had stopped using psychedelic drugs. I wanted to live a more "pure" lifestyle. But I'd tucked away some windowpane LSD—an extremely potent psychedelic—in my hatband, thinking it might come in handy for bartering.

That little stash turned out to be our ticket into the local culture. I asked Keoli if he knew what acid was. He said yes—he was familiar with LSD.

I offered him a couple of windowpanes, which he eagerly accepted—and immediately popped into his mouth.

This was a large overdose of LSD. Half a windowpane was enough to send you into another spiritual dimension for hours— full supernatural technicolor!

Keoli sat in that rocking chair for eight hours straight, eyes glazed, never moving. As I watched him rocking under the influence of that powerful psychedelic, I got really nervous. I started thinking maybe I hadn't escaped that hippie beating after all!

But the amazing thing was—after he finally came down from his eight-hour trip to another world—he came over and thanked me!

The house belonged to his uncle, John Hale (pronounced *Holly*), who was from a famous Hawaiian family with political connections. He was a pure-blood Hawaiian—and a giant of a man. He was so big, his big toe looked about the size of a regular foot!

Becoming friends with this family opened doors for us that were absolutely amazing.

To go from being afraid of the Hawaiians to being accepted by them was a milestone in our journey.

They helped us find a place to stay near Pohoiki and introduced us to people who would make a difference in our lives in Hawaii. They protected us and allowed us to be part of their world.

Instead of being beaten—or possibly killed—for being 'dirty hippies,' we were now being befriended and protected. For the first time in Hawaii, I felt like maybe this Eden could actually be home. I had no idea how quickly paradise would unravel.

CHAPTER THIRTEEN

PARADISE ISN'T WHAT YOU THINK

After a few weeks in Pohoiki, Leah and I started to explore the land around us. The whole area bore the scars of recent eruptions, where the island had literally grown by hundreds of acres. It felt raw, like the earth was still catching its breath.

The a'ā lava stretched out in black deserts, sharp and broken, a jumble of glass-like rock that could slice your feet to ribbons if you weren't careful. We were barefoot most of the time, but you didn't cross 'a'ā barefoot—not if you wanted to keep your soles intact.

Then there was the pāhoehoe lava, different altogether. It had poured out of the volcano in thick ribbons that cooled into smooth, rippling flows. You could walk across it more easily, and in the sunlight, it shimmered with rainbow hues, like oil on water. It was beautiful, but treacherous too—the crust could be thin in spots, and if it gave way, the sharp edges below were waiting.

One afternoon, our wandering brought us into a strange kind of forest. At first glance, it looked like trees, but as we stepped closer, we realized they weren't trees at all. They were stone.

Black, hollow columns rising where the forest had once stood. When lava swept through here, the moisture inside the trunks cooled it on contact, hardening around the trees until the wood inside burned away. What was left were eerie silhouettes—lava trees, the locals called them. The Hawaiians said the place was haunted, and they didn't go there. Walking among them, I could understand why.

Much of the volcanic violence here had happened in 1960, when the Kapoho vent opened. The eruption buried an entire village—hot springs and all—beneath oceans of lava. Now it looked like a moonscape: brown and black stretches of rock, broken only by cinder cones scattered across the fields.

And then, in the middle of that desolation, rose a miracle. A green mountain several hundred feet high, like an island surrounded by a black sea of lava. Around its base, Japanese farmers had carved out flat plots and filled them with orchids. Acres of white and pink blossoms, spread in neat rectangles, blooming defiantly against the lava. To come out of that stark landscape and suddenly see a carpet of orchids—it was quite beautiful.

On my daily treks, foraging for food, I'd sometimes stop to chat with the Japanese farmers and Hawaiians who worked the land around Kapoho. My curiosity always got the better of me, so I asked them about the little green mountain rising out of the lava field. Their answers were brief, almost evasive. Haunted, they said. *Kapu*. Forbidden. No one went there.

That only made me want to go more.

I decided to investigate this mysterious green mountain and made the trek across the lava to the base of the mountain. Up close, the first obstacle wasn't the climb—it was the grass. It grew higher than my head, a razor-sharp wall that cut at my arms and face with every step. I swung my machete, hacking out a path, sweat pouring down until I was drenched. Every foot forward cost me something—scratches, stings, and more sweat.

The slope itself was brutal. There was no trail, just a tangled jungle of vines and brush, and I had to fight for every inch. The air was heavy, close, and by the time I reached the ridge, my body was scratched raw, and my clothes plastered to me. But what I found at the top was absolutely amazing.

The mountain wasn't just a hill—it was a dormant volcanic crater—a perfect bowl, hundreds of feet deep, rimmed by a dense tangle of trees and vines. The walls were sheer columns of volcanic rock, geometric like giant stair-steps, and in every crack, thick brush had rooted.

It would not be an easy climb to the bottom. Using the vines as ropes, I lowered myself from ledge to ledge. The walls were columned rock—giant stair-steps. The air was damp, heavy with the smell of mold. Moss spread over the rocks in green carpets, and patches of bright red and yellow lichen glowed like paint splashed on the stone.

Great webs spanned the shade; in their centers, large, iridescent yellow spiders waited patiently for their dinner. At the bottom, the terrain leveled into a small meadow, still and strange, wrapped in the silence of stone walls and the thick, humid air. It felt like I had stepped into another world. And the more I explored, the more I knew—that's precisely what it was. The island had hidden away a secret world inside itself.

The mongooses scattered at my approach, and everywhere I looked, life was bursting out of the ground. Banana trees sagged under the weight of ripe yellow fruit. Avocado branches bent low, heavy with green orbs. I was ecstatic—bananas and avocados made up most of our daily diet, and here they were, free for the taking. It was like the land itself had been waiting for us, laying out a feast.

The deeper I went, the more impossible it seemed. Oranges and grapefruits hung like lanterns, passion fruit tangled through the brush, breadfruit trees swayed under ten-pound globes of custard-like fruit. Strawberry guavas perfumed the air. Even bamboo stood all around, some slender and some giant, their stalks whispering in the wind.

And then I saw it: a freshwater lake, dark and mysterious, with fish rising to the surface in the afternoon light. I couldn't believe it —Eden had its own water supply.

Up until now, Leah and I had survived on whatever fruits we could gather from the jungle, plus a small stash of nuts, grains, and the medicinal herbs I carried. Our Hawaiian friends sometimes offered us fish, but I was a strict vegan back then—nothing with a face. I had no desire to add another lifetime to my karmic wheel, though I'd soon realize the futility of that thinking.

Most of our meals were raw, eaten out of wooden bowls with spoons we carried in our packs. Alongside them: a saucepan, a machete, a sharp knife, fire-making supplies, a tent, and sleeping bags. I was lean—very lean—but strong, and I swam in Pohoiki Bay whenever the water was calm enough. Our shack sat next to a volcanic hot pool, and we soaked there often, easing our weary bodies.

But stumbling onto this hidden Shangri-La changed everything. Before, we spent hours every day scratching food out of the forest. Now, here it was, all at once—abundant, overflowing, and ours for the gathering.

After that first brutal trek and the discovery of this oasis, I made my way back down the mountain and brought Leah with me into the crater. In the weeks that followed, I found better ways in and out—trails that spared me the machete battle and the bleeding ankles. It became almost idyllic—birds calling from every branch, mongooses darting quickly and shyly through the underbrush.

I ate so much ripe breadfruit—sweet as custard when it's ready —that to this day, I can't look at one without my stomach turning. Avocados became a staple, along with bananas of every kind— plantains, apple bananas, big yellow clusters that seemed to ripen overnight. The oranges in that crater were something else—huge, bursting with juice, sweeter than anything I've ever tasted since. Add in the strawberry guavas, ripe starfruit, passion fruit climbing the vines—you'd think, what more could anyone want?

It was a Garden of Eden.

But I soon discovered that an easy, beautiful environment wasn't a magic formula for happiness. I had, in a way, turned myself into a celibate monk. Leah—young, vibrant, just nineteen— wasn't ready for that kind of life. She loved the adventure, loved getting away from freeways and fast-food jobs in the Bay Area. For her, the move to Hawaii, the idea of living off the land, had been an exciting escape for a middle-class girl raised in a Jewish family.

But the path of denial I was pursuing was not exactly fun. Maybe I hadn't realized—or perhaps I'd chosen to forget—that this young hippie girl just wanted to live, to have fun. I had found her living the whole hippie lifestyle—"If it feels good, do it." Sex, drugs, and rock 'n' roll—that was the theology of the day. And none of that existed in the crater on Green Mountain. I guess I was pretty thick... or maybe caught up in some messiah complex, thinking I could show her a higher way. I missed her when she returned to California.

What we didn't know was that Leah had been exposed to hepatitis. While we were in the crater, she grew very sick, with hepatitis, likely worsened by our diet. With great difficulty, I got her out of the crater and into a hospital. Soon after, she returned to the mainland to recover at her parents' home.

I spent a lot of time alone on Green Mountain. Strange as it sounds, I never saw another soul up there. I came and went as I pleased, and nobody ever stopped me or asked what I was doing. The Japanese orchid farmers who worked the fields at the base would give me a wave as I passed, sometimes even a ride when I was hitching through the Puna district. Over time, I got to know a few of them. They were kind men, most of them Buddhists, and they were fascinated by this long-haired, bearded white guy wandering barefoot in a *lavalava* (a colored cloth wrapped around the waist), following the path of dharma. We'd have conversations about Buddhism and mysticism, and they were curious why I, of all people, had chosen that road. I must have looked like an odd sight to them.

But let me tell you—living alone in "paradise" isn't what people imagine. Having all your physical needs met doesn't mean you're content. The sameness of each day starts to wear on you, like time itself is standing still. To break the monotony, I swam in the lake at the bottom of the crater almost every afternoon.

That lake was its own mystery. The water was dark. Cloudy, with dead trees leaning over the edge, their branches hanging over the surface. Mist often hovered there, giving it an eerie, haunted feel. I'll be honest—it took some courage to dive in the first time, trying to silence the thought that some prehistoric monster might be lurking under the gray surface.

But it was full of life. Schools of mullet darted just below, flashing silver. That told me Hawaiians had once lived here, because mullet didn't just appear by chance. Across the Puna district, the ancients had built fishponds wherever they found water, raising mullet and planting taro as staples. Sure enough, taro plants still grew around the lake's edge, silent evidence of those who had cultivated this place long before me.

I realized then—I wasn't the first to call this crater home.

The reality of living in the Puna district became clearer with every passing week. What drew me there—the warm climate and the abundance of fruit—was also what wore me down. The rain didn't fall; it hammered. Nothing dried. At times, I felt like I was starting to mold. Days on end, I'd be trapped in my shelter, the gray sky pressing low, no sun to break through, and even stepping outside to pee felt like I might drown in the deluge.

And then there was the loneliness. Silence, meditation, navel-gazing—it only took me so far before I found myself going kind of nuts. Having nothing but birds and mongooses for company gives you way too much time to realize how little you know yourself. I tried to fill the hours with reading, shelter-building, anything. But in the end, I was starving for conversation, companionship, for someone else to stir my curiosity and meet me in thought. After all, we were created for relationship.

I would often find myself shouting into the sky, demanding answers from the One I somehow knew was there. Sometimes with a fist raised, sometimes with a desperate plea: *Why am I here? Why am I alive, conscious, aware?* It seemed that perhaps He couldn't hear me, even though I couldn't conceive of that being true.

I had invested so much of my time and energy into my "cosmic glue" philosophy. But here in this volcanic crater, my search for

God-consciousness was failing me. My groceries, my meditations, my fastings, my denials of worldly comforts—they weren't getting me any closer to what I was searching for. And yet the reality of His being was all around me, and I could feel Him deep inside my soul, hidden in a place I couldn't reach on my own. The harder I tried, the more that awareness slipped from my grasp.

But maybe that was the message all along.

He wasn't hiding behind my striving. He wasn't waiting on the other side of enlightenment or asceticism. He was already here. Inside. Present in a way I couldn't earn, hidden in plain sight.

And maybe... just maybe... I hadn't been the seeker after all. Perhaps He was the one calling out to me.

CHAPTER FOURTEEN
GUAVA KARMA

Life itself is such irony. The very things we do to change who we are—the things we work so hard to fix—often betray us. I learned that one night in the jungles of Puna, in living color.

I was trying to escape the endless wheel of birth, death, and rebirth. The only way off, so I believed, was to rid myself of bad karma. So I became a strict vegetarian—no animal products, no killing of any living thing. Not a centipede, not a mosquito. Through meditation, pure foods, good works, and self-denial, I thought I could shed karmic guilt and finally unite with the Godhead.

During my fruit-foraging trips around the Puna district, I was allowed to camp on a friend's property in the jungle. My tent was pitched beside a trail that wound through the forest. I was alone, just soaking in the beauty of the jungle—so alive, so full of life.

That evening, under the light of a full moon, I decided to take a walk down the trail and experience the solitude and beauty all around me. The air was fragrant with flowers, the trees forming a thick canopy overhead, and the path was lined with guava bushes heavy with ripe fruit.

I was ecstatic! It felt like the universe had laid a feast before me.

I ate guavas. Oh, how I ate guavas. I don't think I've ever enjoyed any fruit as much as I enjoyed those guavas that night. So different from life back in the world, with its endless struggle and pressure to make a living, to live life by the clock and daily schedule. After my moonlit walk, I returned to my camp and settled in for the night, feeling deeply satisfied—and favored.

At dawn, I returned to the trail for more. Sunlight streamed through the trees as I plucked the first guava, bit in, and froze.

To my horror, every guava I picked was crawling with tiny, white maggots—every one of them. In the soft moonlight, I hadn't seen them, but I had devoured them by the handful.

The realization hit me like a ton of bricks. No matter how hard I sacrificed, no matter how carefully I worked to get off that damned wheel of death and life, I was doomed to failure.

Back to the cosmic karmic drawing board, I guess. How many times would I have to die and be reincarnated to make up for the hundreds of innocent maggots I'd unknowingly eaten—sending them to their deaths in a pool of stomach acid?

Life is ironic.

Was Someone trying to tell me something?

The cracks were showing in my Dharma road—the so-called right way of living. Someone, somewhere, was speaking to me.

The real question was, *was I ready to listen?* Because sometimes reality is like a mule kick to the head.

CHAPTER FIFTEEN
TIME FOR A CHANGE

During my time in Puna, I got to know a kind couple who lived on the land near Kapoho, not far from where I was camping. I'll call them Fred and June. They often picked me up when I was hitchhiking around the area. They said they were Christians, and they showed us a lot of kindness.

They were from the mainland, and a few years earlier had bought land in Hawaii to live off the grid. Their organic farm was thriving—vegetables they sold in Pahoa or shared with the local hippies. Warm and friendly, Fred and June became like a mom-and-pop substitute for wandering souls, offering not just food but comfort and advice.

Throughout Puna, many folks had embraced the hippie, counterculture, back-to-the-land lifestyle. They were living simple lives without electricity or modern conveniences. I was one of them. But after months in the jungle, reality was closing in on me. My grains and nuts were gone, and I was down to bananas and avocados. Believe it or not, it could get really chilly in Hawaii, and

I needed clothes. The constant wet made it impossible to stay dry. It was clear—I needed work, money, and a change. The "universe" didn't dispense cash.

About that time, Leah returned from the mainland, where she'd been recovering from hepatitis. She'd stayed with her parents in the Bay Area until she was strong enough to travel, and now she was back. But there was no way I could take her into the jungle again—not with the constant rain and dampness that could seep into your bones. She needed sunshine, warmth, and time to heal. It was clear that the season of jungle living had run its course.

It was time to rejoin the world. Or, as we used to call it back then, Babylon—modern, workaday society.

As we spent more time with Fred and June, they introduced us to their friends James and Molly, who lived in Pahoa. They generously offered us a spot in their basement with access to a bathroom and kitchen. We gladly accepted, though I had trepidation. When I'd left the Bay Area, I'd burned a lot of bridges —walking away from the smog, the noise, the abuse of the earth. Now I was moving back into society, even if it was just a small Hawaiian town. I had to eat some serious crow.

So Leah and I packed our few possessions, stuck out our thumbs, and hitched into Pahoa—leaving the Puna coast and Green Mountain behind.

James and Molly weren't into Eastern religion like so many others we knew. They called themselves Christians. Their home was a hub for weekly Bible studies, drawing hippies, drifters, and seekers who showed up for food, showers, and fellowship. I didn't join. I figured I was too spiritually advanced for that kind of thing. I'd left behind the Christianity of my childhood, with all its talk of heaven, hell, and a bloody cross.

Still, James and Molly's kindness stood out. They weren't pushy or judgmental—just generous. Their doors were open to barefoot hippies, organic mamas, and wandering seekers who came through grateful for a hot meal or a dry bed. Leah and I fit right in. But living there full-time meant we weren't just guests— we were part of the household, helping with meals, cleaning, and caring for whoever passed through.

I had long talks with the "traveling space cowboys" about everything under the sun. Because I knew about plant-based diets and herbs, people constantly asked me health questions. Many were struggling with malnutrition—protein deficiencies from poor diets. But the most common problem by far was staph infections. A mosquito bite or a cut could turn nasty fast, and herbal poultices rarely touched it.

One of the young guys who came through the house—a strikingly handsome Californian of Japanese ancestry—showed up with full-blown staph. His face was covered in sores from infected bites, spreading fast. I'd seen enough staph in the service to know how dangerous it could get. I told him he needed antibiotics. He refused, convinced he'd heal with herbs. Day by day, the sores got worse, eating into his skin, leaving deep pits. Finally, after weeks of useless leaves and desperation, he gave in and took antibiotics. They killed the infection, but the scars were permanent.

This was one of the really sad things I witnessed among so many hippies: a stubbornness not to use modern medicine, no matter the failures of herbs to heal, and ignorance of basic nutritional laws. It was common among the hundreds of young people looking for the Garden of Eden—a zeal, but no knowledge.

Pahoa itself was a unique town of a few thousand people, supported mainly through sugarcane and large orange groves. The shops and stores had a strong presence from both Filipino and Japanese cultures. Some of the local hippies grew marijuana—*pakalolo*, the "crazy weed"—and it brought them a steady income. Many of the Hawaiians, Filipinos, and Japanese worked in the cane fields, and others at the mill just outside town. The mill ran day and night, billowing steam from tall chimneys, the smell of molasses heavy in the air like a wet blanket. The town looked like something out of the Old West—narrow main street, wooden sidewalks, false-front buildings, even a 25-cent theater. The house we stayed in was just on the edge of town, on the road that led back toward Kapoho and the rest of the Puna district.

Our first night in the basement—which was open on one side—I was jolted awake by bright lights that made the night seem like day and the sound of giant machines, a deafening racket of grinding gears and squeaking wheels. For a moment, it felt like they were coming straight through our room. These were the sugarcane harvesters—gigantic machines with floodlights blazing, operators sitting high in cockpits, levers clanking as they chewed through the fields. The harvest ran non-stop, day and night, until every last stalk was cut. It was like trying to sleep in the middle of an industrial war zone. Then suddenly, after days of chaos, it was over. The fields stood bare, the machines were gone, and we finally got some peace.

Life in Pahoa was a far cry from the quiet serenity of my crater in Green Mountain. But here there were people—faces, conversations, stories. The young pilgrims who came through reminded me of myself when I first landed in the Puna district—wide-eyed, chasing Eden. They weren't prepared for the endless rain, the gloom, or the quiet hostility from some of the locals who saw us long-haired, tie-dyed kids as invaders of their ancestral home. They had no idea what they were stepping into.

What I didn't expect was how much I would appreciate my conversations with James and Molly. We came from different worlds—me with my Buddhist leanings, them with their Christian faith—but our talks were never unpleasant. Always respectful. Always real. And their belief in Christ wasn't just talk; it showed up in how they lived, how they loved, how they served people who had nothing to offer in return.

That stuck with me.

Their faith moved me in a way I couldn't dismiss. There was a small voice inside me that kept turning it over, refusing to let me walk away from it completely. I found myself thinking about James and Molly more than I ever expected—their kindness, their peace, their God.

There were so many stories of my time in Puna—some beautiful, some hard to explain. But not all of it felt like the heart of what I was chasing. I could feel it stirring in me—that need for something new. I'd had my fill of quiet jungle mornings, barefoot philosophies, and the dream of Eden. I was ready for sun and dry ground. Kona called.

But before that, I had a few more things to face. I still needed to make some money. I wasn't quite done with Babylon just yet.

CHAPTER SIXTEEN
SHOVELING SAND IN BABYLON

I caught a ride to the job site to meet the man hiring a laborer. Portuguese—heavyset, dark hair, beady eyes. Gruff. Not friendly. He didn't ask any questions, just barked: Show up tomorrow.

So I did. Hitched a ride ten miles toward Hilo and found myself staring at a mountain of sand—ten feet high, thirty feet across. The boss shoved a shovel in my hands and pointed to a gas-powered hopper. The machine blasted sand through a hose and nozzle at high pressure, stripping rust from diesel truck frames.

It was brutal.

For months, I'd been walking, swimming, and eating papayas and bananas. Not exactly training for industrial labor. Lean from a low-protein diet, unprepared for what this job demanded—ninety degrees, humidity near 100%. I was drenched in sweat before I lifted the shovel. My job was simple: keep the hopper full so the nozzle operator never ran dry. That meant relentless shoveling—sometimes an hour at a time without a break—until he stopped.

I worked in shorts and sneakers. By the end of the first day, I was burned, soaked, gritty, and every muscle screamed with cramps. It was the most punishing work I had ever done—pure torture. Now I understood why the boss needed help—nobody lasted. I managed about a week before I hit my limit. Not lazy— but I wasn't stupid either. It was a miracle I didn't end up in the hospital with heat stroke.

When I told him I couldn't do it anymore, he exploded—called me a worthless bastard, a lazy hippie. I didn't care. No mere mortal could survive that job for long. He promised to pay me if I came back the next day. I did. And the next. And the next. But he never showed. I never got paid. The hardest job I ever did—and I got stiffed. Later, I heard that was his trick. Burn through guys like me, promise pay, disappear.

That was my re-entry into Babylon—work schedules, bosses, pay that never came. It wasn't pretty.

I picked up odd jobs here and there to help cover our share of the house expenses. But something had shifted. Deep inside, I could feel it. There was a stirring—a subtle inner prompting. Like something was guiding my steps. A change was coming. I could feel it in my bones.

A word before we continue—in a personal memoir, the main character—me, in this case—is supposed to be the good guy. But as I write, looking back across the years, I see it differently. Time pulls the camera back. What once felt noble now looks naïve, sometimes selfish, even ugly.

I want to be honest about those three years in Hawaii, from

January 1971 until May 1974. Really, the story started in '68 in the Bay Area. I wish I could paint myself as the noble seeker, pure-hearted pilgrim. But I wasn't. And the more I remember, the more I see there was someone else—something else—moving beneath the surface. The real hero here isn't me. He's invisible, but He was always there—active, patient, drawing me toward Himself.

With that out of the way, I'll keep going.

There's more to tell. A lot more.

Leah and I had a friendship, but it wasn't love—not in a deep, covenant sense. Our bond started with sexual attraction, passion, lust. I cared for her, but not the way I loved my wife, Jeannie, or the bond I had with my daughter, Annie.

Jeannie and I were still married, though separated—her choice, my stubbornness. By the time I left for Hawaii with Leah, Jeannie had moved on. She started seeing one of my closest childhood friends. Even after separation, I had quit peyote and LSD, but the gulf that unfaithfulness created remained. It is hard to heal and reestablish trust.

Leah and I were traveling the same road—but in different lanes. For her, Hawaii was a fun escape, an adventure—a nineteen-year-old hippie's rebellion. For me, it was something else and far deeper—spiritual searching.

I had no idea how deep I would be taken on this journey of self-awareness, and I didn't know the pain and agony that would be revealed in the years to come. I had given up everything to follow this path—and slowly, it was becoming clear that what I had chosen to abandon might actually be the very reality, the foundation, of what I was seeking.

If I really were walking the dharma road, I had wandered far off its precepts—the ones contained in the Buddhist Eightfold Path. Which, as I now saw it, were nothing more than the same biblical concepts I had learned in Sunday school at the Church of Christ. Precepts like right living, faithfulness, honesty, commitment, putting others first, and seeing reality clearly—all wrapped in Eastern religious and New Age garb.

It was basically the Golden Rule we all grew up with: "Do unto others as you would have them do unto you"—even if you weren't particularly religious.

It seemed to me that I had confused the outward signs of Buddhism—fasting, self-denial, meditation, strict dietary laws, and withdrawing from society—with its actual purpose and spirit, which was true spiritual transformation. A way to inner peace and union with truth, whoever—or whatever—that turned out to be. I had missed the point.

And at the center of all my searching was me—a selfish narcissist.

It's a painful thing when truth or reality finally kicks you hard in the ass.

What I'm trying to say is simple... *I really, really missed my wife and daughter.* My mind and heart kept returning to them. They mattered more than cosmic consciousness or spiritual enlightenment. It had been over six months since I left, and I was growing homesick and heartsick for Jeannie and my little Michelle Ann Marie Land—*Annie.*

I remembered the inscription inside my wedding ring: *All my love. All my life.* I'm not by nature a very sentimental guy. I don't remember birthdays or holidays, and I don't care if anyone celebrates mine. But those memories haunted me. I wanted to get back to Jeannie and Annie.

Maybe—just maybe—there was still a chance for a second chance for us. And for that, I was willing to return to Babylon to find out.

PART FOUR
BETWEEN WORLDS

"I wasn't home in Hawaii, and I wasn't home in Babylon. I was somewhere in between—adrift, restless, undone. Yet even there, the Presence remained."

CHAPTER SEVENTEEN
THE RETURN

In the middle of 1971, I found myself on a plane heading back to the San Francisco Bay Area. I was leaving the Big Island of Hawaii to return to California—to see my daughter Annie and my wife Jeannie. When I left for Hawaii in January, I had no intention of returning, so this was definitely a deviation from my plans. But in reality, I hadn't made any plans at all—I just left. I walked away from the pollution and chaos of the Bay Area, chasing that elusive answer to the questions that never stopped percolating in my heart and mind.

As I stared out the airplane window, watching clouds pass around us, I was tangled up inside. All I could see were giant question marks about this decision to return.

Over the next four and a half hours, a mix of emotions swirled inside me—anticipation and excitement, anxiety and fear—as I thought about seeing Jeannie and Annie for the first time in six months.

As we started our descent into San Francisco International

Airport, I could feel my heart begin to race as I heard and felt the loud clunk of the wheels as they were lowered and the roar as they touched the airport runway. I had flown hundreds of thousands of miles on aircraft in my past on my trips back and forth from the USA to Japan and hitching rides on Navy transport planes visiting the cities of Japan. I didn't mind flying; I had actually taught myself to fall asleep as soon as the plane took off, but I always really hated the landings. My heart would always beat faster, and I would squeeze the armrests with my fingers a little more tightly.

But this time, the nerves weren't about the landing. I was anxious about the unknown. I had no idea how I'd be received—by Jeannie, by Annie, by all those I'd abruptly left behind. As I stepped off the plane and made my way to baggage claim, I was nervous, not knowing what to expect.

I had arranged to be picked up by a dear friend named Nina—a close friend of both Jeannie and me, someone we shared a deep history with. At one point, Nina, her husband Phil, and their daughter Lily had even lived with us in our apartment, back when Jeannie and I were still together, shortly before our separation. Eventually, Nina and Phil divorced—just like Jeannie and I did. The reasons were all too familiar: infidelity, incompatible lifestyles, and the psychedelic drug scene.

Jeannie had actually thrown me out of the house, so it was easy to put the blame on her, although I knew that I had provoked her and was the cause of the breakup.

After I left for Hawaii, Jeannie, her sister Janet, Annie, Nina, and Lily all moved into an old Victorian house in a little town called Crockett, perched near the water on the Carquinez Strait in the North Bay.

The fact that these women ended up renting a house together in Crockett was one of those 'you can't make this stuff up' moments.

Crockett, California, was a sugar town. Its entire purpose was to produce pure cane sugar from Hawaiian molasses. Ships from places like Pāhoa and Hilo would dock regularly, unloading hundreds of thousands of gallons of pungent molasses from the very islands I had just left.

Jeannie and Nina graciously invited me to stay in their Victorian home, which, in itself, was more than a little surprising. There was no animosity, no lingering bitterness. It was strange, honestly. I expected tension, maybe even hostility. But instead, the women welcomed me with kindness.

Even Nina—with whom I'd once had a romantic relationship —had moved on. They all had. And wanted me to move on with mine.

Each day, I'd gaze out the window of the old Victorian, which overlooked the massive C&H Sugar plant, and my mind would drift back to Pāhoa and its endless fields of sugarcane. I remembered the glaring bright lights of the great harvest machines, the sleepless nights as they worked the fields around the clock, and the all-pervasive smell of cane being heated and molasses extracted.

Now, in the little town of Crockett, I woke and slept to the same pungent scent of cooking molasses. In my mind, I was no longer two thousand miles from Hilo. I could feel the warm, humid air again. Smell the thick, damp jungle of Puna. I knew I would go back.

My reason for returning to the Bay Area had been twofold: I missed my daughter Annie desperately. At two and a half years old, she was growing so fast, and I couldn't bear another day apart. And I still carried a faint hope of reconciliation with Jeannie. I knew the chances were slim. But I had to try at least.

I settled into the routine around the house. Household chores were divided fairly among all of us. It was a happy household. Nina worked as a tax preparer and had clients who sometimes came by the house; other times, she'd travel to meet them. Jeannie worked at a medical clinic, and her sister Janet was a student. Together, they created a healthy, stable home for the two children —Annie and Lily (Nina's daughter).

Living with Jeannie and Annie again, even if I was just another housemate to Jeannie, felt incredibly good. I was soaking up every moment I had with Annie. She was overjoyed to have me back in her world—constantly by my side, laughing, holding my hand, full of love. I know she was hoping her mom and I might get back together. That hope was at the forefront of my thoughts, too.

One day, while we were spending time together, Annie said something very strange and threw me for a loop.

"I have two daddies," she said. "You and one that comes to me at night sits by my bed and says he loves me. Is that you too?"

My mind went back to those long hours meditating in the volcano crater in Hawaii. Often, I would imagine my spirit traveling to Crockett—to Annie's room—where I'd sit quietly beside her bed, stroke her hair, and whisper how much I loved her.

It was shocking. Annie described exactly what I had imagined in the crater. How could she know? I don't know, except that my love and desire to be near her was so strong that it created a reality. Love finds a way, I believe that.

I needed to find work soon to help with the rent and household expenses. After some searching, I landed a job at Adachi's Nursery—one of the oldest in California, initially founded by the Adachi family in Southern California. Hideo Adachi ran the branch I worked for in the north.

Hideo was a great guy to work for. I think my basic knowledge of Japanese helped me land the job—he loved hearing me speak my version of Japanese and would often laugh at my pronunciation. The nursery was well-known and successful, and I stayed busy tending to the endless variety of flowers and plants. I genuinely loved the work.

Now keep in mind, I was still a long-haired, bearded hippie— and still very organic-minded. So, every time Hideo sprayed the nursery with insecticides or herbicides, I gave him grief. I'd rant about poisons and chemicals, insisting there had to be a better, more natural way.

Eventually, Hideo had had enough. With a sly grin, he told me, "Okay, we do it your way." He stopped spraying entirely—not to agree with me, but to teach me a lesson that he knew what he was doing.

Two weeks later, he asked me to inspect the plants and report back. I walked through the nursery, lifting leaves and examining stems—and what I found horrified me. The undersides of the leaves were crawling with whiteflies. Aphids clung to the stems. The plants looked sick, drooping, and stressed.

Hideo asked me what I had found and to give him my report. I was embarrassed and a little afraid I had cost him money. It was obvious that my all-natural, no chemical, all-organic theories didn't impress my boss. Hideo didn't say a word. He just got up, prepared the spray rig, handed me a mask, and told me to start spraying.

I was surprised that Hideo didn't fire me, but he never mentioned it again. As the months progressed, I would again and again be forced to eat huge helpings of humble pie. It was obvious that I didn't have the universe figured out, and in reality, I never would figure it out in my mind or by reading or searching in New Age philosophy. It took a few more years before I would meet the face behind eternity.

After a few weeks of settling into the Crockett house, I finally worked up the courage to ask Jeannie if we could talk alone. After I left, Jeannie was not one to spend endless hours moping and feeling sorry for herself. She immediately landed on her feet and began her new life. I seemed to be the needy one, and I needed to know where we stood. While I'd been gone, she had dated a few guys, but lately, she'd been seeing someone regularly—an old friend of mine, Stephen, whom I'd known since the fourth grade. Back in high school, Jeannie and I would frequently double-date with him and his girlfriend. Now, they were spending a lot of time together, and it had me worried. I hoped it wasn't too late for us.

I was nervous about it. I'm sure Stephen had his fears too, wondering if Jeannie would choose to come back to me. She and I walked down the hall to a back bedroom, with Annie trailing close behind. When we stepped into the room, Annie gently closed the door behind us. I'll never forget her sweet face—those eyes full of hope.

It was the first time Jeannie and I had been alone together since our separation. My heart was pounding. I was sweaty, clammy, and unsure just thinking about asking her to consider forgiving me and restoring our marriage. What could I say? My apologies seemed so weak. I tried to explain how much I loved her and what a big mistake I had made by not valuing our marriage. I felt real pain in my guts as I realized how mindless my apologies sounded. I was exposed in my shallowness and stupidity. In my mind, this whole thing was going worse than I had ever thought possible. At that moment, I realized how deeply I had wounded Jeannie.

Then she spoke. Her words surprised me.

She said she still loved me—had always loved me—and that nothing I'd done or would do could ever change that. But she couldn't live with me again as my wife. After I left, Stephen had been there for her. He'd walked with her through the pain, through the loneliness. She couldn't turn around now and leave him to come back to me. He wasn't strong enough to endure being rejected, she said. She didn't know how he'd survive it. He was deeply in love with her. But me? I was strong, a survivor. I'd be fine. Believe me, she was giving me way too much credit. At that moment, I felt weak and broken. As Jeannie spoke these words, any hopes I had were completely crushed.

We embraced tightly for a long time, and both wept deeply with sobs and tears. I realized too late what I'd lost. And that was it. Basically, she told me she couldn't do to Stephen what I had done to her.

The door was closed.

There it was—I was hoisted on my own spear. And man, did it

hurt. The finality of her decision hit like a punch to the gut—a deep, physical ache.

I once heard it said: You can pretend to avoid reality, but you can't escape the consequences of it. Well, now reality had hit me square in the face—or maybe more accurately, in the heart.

And now what?

For the next few weeks, I was an emotional wreck. I was feeling the full weight of my choices—a heavy, ugly weight I could hardly bear.

Even though it was hard for both Jeannie and me—sensing the pain and finality of her decision—we all continued living together in Crockett. And for that brief season, it was wonderful to be with Annie every day. But I knew it wouldn't last forever.

I sank into a deep depression. For weeks, I could barely function. Jeannie and Nina, trying to help, invited an old friend over—someone we'd all known for years. They hoped that she might cheer me up. Remember, this was the era of free love and sexual liberation. The idea was that a bit of companionship might snap me out of it. Get my mind off my troubles.

It didn't.

All desire—emotional, physical, even social—had left me. I was too wrecked. I couldn't receive the more than generous offer of a friendly, sexual relationship with this would-be angel of mercy. I was numb. These gals really felt sorry for me that they couldn't get me out of my deep emotional slump. I was just going through the motions, not truly living, not enjoying life at all. My only ray of happiness was Annie. Her love and presence were my connection with the reality that love in my world still existed.

I wasn't making enough at the nursery, so I applied for a job in Albany—almost an hour away from Crockett. It was night shift at a factory that made 2,000-pound rolls of paper tape. The pay was solid, and I could finally get a full 40-hour week.

This new job really helped give me a different perspective and viewpoint on life. For me, it was a grand distraction.

My job? Cooking glue. Hundreds of gallons of it. In giant steel pots.

I'd climb a ladder and dump in 100-pound bags of dry glue—made from dead cow hooves and animal gelatin. I'd watch it bubble and boil, then coat the paper tape as it ran through rollers, heaters, and back again, until it wound into 2,000-pound finished rolls.

The smell? Absolutely foul. Overpowering.

And there I was—a former Buddhist vegetarian—making glue from dead cows. How far I had fallen.

My cosmic world was turned upside down.

But the people at my job? That was the best part. Truly a redeeming factor in this crazy drama.

I worked with a great bunch of guys from different ethnic backgrounds, and we laughed a lot during breaks. We really enjoyed each other's company. Most of them were Mexican Americans and Black guys. They teased me about my long hair and vegan diet—but it was all good-natured and full of laughter.

We'd banter and tease each other as we played dominoes on break. They'd brag about their romantic conquests. One of the guys, an older African American man getting ready to retire, used to tease me that I'd never have a Black girlfriend—joking that what Black women had to offer sexually was way too rich for a white boy like me. He had us rolling.

I loved those guys. I realized how blessed I was to be working with them.

And yet... as I ran the machines, my thoughts would drift. Just a short while ago, I was living the "natural" life—eating fruit and vegetables straight from the land, no clock to punch, no one to answer to. I came and went as I pleased. I'd left behind "Babylon" —the 9-to-5 grind, the trappings of middle-class America.

I used to laugh at the people still trapped in it.

Now... I was one of them.

Here I was—back in Babylon. Punching a time clock. Living the middle-class lifestyle I used to mock. I still looked like a hippie —long hair, beard, tie-dyes—but inside, cataclysmic changes had overtaken me. I was deep in soul-searching mode, and I knew I would never be satisfied living this way.

Life has a way of shifting on a dime. One moment things feel stable, and the next, everything's different. Overwhelming, even. But it's in those moments that I started to see it— *Someone* was leading me. I could feel it. I didn't know where or what was waiting, but I knew I was headed somewhere.

I'd mocked Babylon. Now I was living in it, punching a time clock, and breathing chemicals, cooking glue out of dead cows. And yet, deep inside, I could feel it—my cosmic glue wasn't holding anymore. Whatever was out there wasn't just a force. It was Someone. And He wasn't going to leave me alone.

CHAPTER EIGHTEEN
THE CALL

Sometimes, it only takes a phone call to change your whole life.

One ring, and everything shifts.

You think you're headed in one direction, and then—**bam**—your life takes a turn you never saw coming.

Something so bizarre it boggles your mind.

The phone rang.

It was Leah, calling from Hilo. I could tell right away—something was wrong. She wasn't hysterical, but she was clearly upset. I asked what was going on, what she needed.

She said, "John... I'm pregnant. I'm alone. I don't want to have an abortion. Please... come back to Hawaii and help me with this pregnancy. I can't do this by myself."

Her words hit like a blow. It sent me reeling. What was I to do?

Should I go back? Was it even my place? After all, I was the one who brought her to Hawaii. I had left her—but only because she *wanted* to stay. She had been so sure. But now? She was scared. Alone. And I cared about her.

I knew what I had to do. I had to go back.

Let me rewind for a moment—back to just before I left Hilo for the Bay Area.

I had picked up work with a couple from New York, Michael and Zipporah, who decided they wanted to "be hippies." Trouble was, they didn't want to give up their wealth or comfort. They had the tie-dye shirts, bell-bottoms, long hair, and plenty of pakalolo—the best money could buy—but underneath it all, Michael was still proud of being a slumlord. He actually bragged about collecting rent from poor tenants and never fixing a thing. That left a bad taste in my mouth. He didn't get it. Peace and love weren't about milking people.

We stayed in one of Michael's basements—damp, dark, but it was a roof over our heads. In exchange for rent and a few bucks, I built oak tables, poured resin, sanded, worked faithfully and diligently to help him open his pizza parlor downtown. Kau Kau Korner, he called it.

What really stuck with me from that season wasn't the work—it was the people I kept running into. Twice a week, without fail, an elderly Japanese couple would stand on the sidewalk outside with a Bible. He in a suit and tie, she in a flowered dress and hat. They didn't shout, didn't condemn. They just quietly, faithfully shared how Jesus had changed their lives—how they'd been Buddhists all their lives until Christ revealed Himself as the God who loved them and forgave them. They made a vow to tell everyone they met, and they kept it. Watching them, so steady and tender, it stirred something in me.

Then, across the street, a group of young people started a Christian bookstore—building shelves, stacking books, full of excitement. They couldn't stop talking about Jesus. Their joy was infectious.

It got under my skin. Everywhere I turned— the student on the steps of the college, Fred and June in Kapoho, James and Molly in Pāhoa, now this Japanese couple and these young bookstore kids—the same thread kept appearing. Love. Not cosmic force, not yin and yang. Love that looked you in the eye and said you mattered. Love that welcomed strangers.

Tommy was a classic California surfer kid—all sun-bleached hair, easy grin, no worries in the world. He helped me at the shop, hauling oak, sanding tables, always laid-back, always good vibes. I introduced Leah to Tommy because she was around the job frequently. I didn't know it then, but after I left for the mainland, they had a brief fling that would change everything for both of us. By the time Leah realized she was pregnant, Tommy was long gone. He never knew.

And now—months later—she was calling me, terrified and alone.

I was ready for a change—even though leaving Annie tore at me in a way nothing else could. But I'd made up my mind. I was going back to Hilo to help Leah with this new life.

I went to my employer, explained the situation, and said my goodbyes to the crew at the factory. When I told them why I was quitting—to help a woman who wasn't my wife, carrying a child that wasn't mine—they thought I was crazy.

"Hippies are nuts," they said.

Maybe they were right. I didn't fully understand it myself.

But something deeper was pulling me. I was being led in this direction. I had to go.

Back in Crockett, I broke the news to Jeannie, Annie, and the women at the house. That conversation with Annie was the hardest. We had rebuilt so much. We were close again. She cried when she realized I was leaving, and I held her tightly—tighter than ever before. I kissed her over and over and over and told her I loved her with all my heart. I promised I'd see her again soon.

At the time, I was hoping that she'd come to visit me in Hawaii. I was blessed when she came over and stayed with me on Lila Farm for a month the following year. That thought—her being with me again—would become one of the things that got me through.

Everyone in the house knew the baby wasn't mine—I'd been away too long for that to be possible. But they also knew Leah. They had met her, seen her heart, and they supported my decision to go. They understood, maybe even better than I did.

The very thought or possibility of Leah getting an abortion settled the issue for me. The idea of her ending that life was something I couldn't accept—not then, not now.

My New Age friends often talked about "masses of tissue," but I saw something else.

A life. A person. A child who deserved to live.

So I booked my flight. Whatever waited for me on the other side would meet me soon enough.

CHAPTER NINETEEN
COMING HOME

As the plane began its descent, I looked out the window and once again marveled at the incredible beauty of Hilo. The first thing that struck me was the endless greens—thousands of shades folding into each other like a living kaleidoscope. Sunlight poured through the canopy, scattering across the jungle in shimmering waves. Who knew green wasn't one color but a thousand? It felt surreal, almost like a Maxwell Parrish painting—too vivid, too magical to be real.

Above it all, a blue sky stretched wide, swollen with clouds ready to burst. And when the rain fell, sunlight broke through the edges and painted the famous rainbows that only Hilo seems to know how to make.

As the plane circled lower, I spotted Hilo Harbor with Coconut Island in the middle of the bay. Memories rushed back—picnics, swims, laughter on the beaches. My love for this island welled up inside me, and I felt the relief of being home again.

The wheels hit the tarmac. The plane stopped. The truth sank in—I was back in Hawaii.

Stepping into the aisle, I moved toward the open door, and the warm breath of Hilo hit me like a hug. Thick, humid air full of life and memory. The scent of the island—earthy, floral, ocean-soaked —wrapped around me. That first inhale said more than words ever could: *You're home.*

I hadn't realized how much I'd missed this place until Hawaiian soil was under my feet again. Even in Crockett, I'd never fully left. Watching those sugar ships unload molasses, smelling it in the air—it was like Hawaii kept whispering through the fog of California. Maybe, in my mind, I had never left.

Leah was waiting at baggage claim. Flip-flops, shorts, a knotted Jamaican shirt, her slim frame already showing the curve of her pregnancy. She'd gotten pregnant almost immediately after I left, so she was a few months along.

Leah was striking—small-framed, fair-skinned, raven hair down her back. Jewish by background, but not orthodox by any means. The only thing Jewish about her anymore was her last name. She'd gone hippie back in high school—sex, drugs, and rock and roll. She rejected religion and Western cultural traditions. She was sexually liberated, and her entire spiritual life consisted of LSD and mescaline psychedelic experiences.

And yet, she wasn't adrift. She worked part-time, took classes at the local college, and floated through life's chaos with a kind of effortless resilience. Carefree, charming, vulnerable in a way that made people want to protect her, especially men. And I was living proof of that—back in Hawaii, helping her carry a pregnancy that wasn't mine.

We left the airport in an old blue van, climbing Waianuenue

Avenue alongside the Wailuku River. We passed Rainbow Falls, rainbows shimmering in the mist, then wound through rolling 'ohia forests and sugar cane fields, the ocean flashing in glimpses below.

Eventually, we turned down a long driveway lined with blooming gardenias. Their scent poured through the open windows—sweet, intoxicating, almost overwhelming. At the end stood a two-story sugar plantation mansion, a broad porch stretching wide, every detail whispering of another era when names like Spreckels and Dole ruled the island.

"How did you land this place?" I asked.

Leah grinned and said a professor at the university owned it. He was leaving on a long trip and had asked her to stay. The fact that he trusted his home to a seemingly carefree hippie was a testament to Leah's uncanny ability to charm just about anyone into just about anything.

Inside, the house was a time capsule of glory—wainscoting, hardwood floors, crown molding, plaster ceilings. And, of course, it had become a hippie commune.

First, there was Billy, tall and blond, dressed in embroidered peasant clothes, dreaming of rock stardom while his girlfriend, Summer Rain, floated around in crystals and tie-dyes. Then Steve and Patti, inseparable, cheerful, and almost "square" compared to the rest.

And then came the gut punch. Michael and Zipporah. The wealthy "hippies" from New York, the very ones I'd worked for at Kau Kau Korner. Now they occupied the master suite, paying the bills, pulling strings. Even here, in a so-called communal paradise, money still ruled, and influence was bought. They used their wealth to sway a household of young hippies with few resources and naïve to the max. I was mortified by it. Michael was greedy, selfish, and, by his own admission, used people for his own advantage. I didn't fit into his scheme, and I didn't want to.

Communal living at the mansion was a challenge, and the mix of personalities, ages, levels of maturity, and values guaranteed conflict.

As news of the mansion reached the hippie population at large in Puna and Hilo, we had a steady stream of transient folks who would stay awhile, then travel through. There was always a variety of hippies and spiritual seekers staying at the mansion.

We were a vegetarian household, and our meals were taken communally. We lived on lentil stews, eggplant parmesan, carrot juice, banana smoothies, and salads piled high with whatever we could gather. We drank so much carrot juice we started turning orange, and we loved lentils—the furry little flying saucer beans—a hippie diet staple.

The smell of weed hung in the air like incense. I rarely smoked pot. It would just make me nervous and paranoid. Drugs held nothing for me, for the most part, they seemed to be the problem and offered no solutions, but most of the folks at the house hadn't reached that point and were still fascinated and captivated by the false hope that psychedelic drugs could unlock secrets of the universe.

CHAPTER TWENTY

NO MORE GURUS

I was trying to help Leah with her pregnancy, so we started going to natural childbirth classes together—Lamaze training, they called it. They taught us how to care for the mother during pregnancy and, when the time came, how to coach her breathing through contractions to prevent pain. The instructors promised that if you did it right, childbirth wasn't pain at all, just "pressure." I never bought that for a minute, and I don't think Leah did either.

So there I was—standing in as her breathing coach, filling the role where usually a husband or father would be. I was, in every sense, a surrogate husband. Leah took her pregnancy seriously and didn't use any drugs, except for the occasional joint. I was proud of her. For all her wildness, she faced motherhood head-on, and I admired that.

At the same time, we began attending transcendental meditation meetings at the University of Hawaii in Hilo, where a popular Indian guru named DaDa G, a disciple of the famous guru BaBa G, was drawing crowds by the hundreds. Spiritual seekers packed into these mass meditation sessions like they were concerts. But from the first time I walked in, I felt uneasy.

DaDa G had this arrogant swagger, this self-satisfied smirk. He would sit in the lotus position and lead his followers in the chanting of "OHM"—the so-called cosmic sound of the universe—rolled through the auditorium like some hypnotic fog. Everyone else seemed entranced. I just felt creeped out.

People treated him like he was more than a man. An avatar. An ascended master. Divine. But I didn't see it.

Then one night after a session, I watched him toss trash on the ground as if it were nothing, and moments later, he brazenly hit on Leah, right in front of me.

That was it. The spell shattered. The whole guru thing collapsed in a single moment of arrogance and disrespect.

No more gurus.

I'd had enough of spiritual salesmen and cosmic con artists. Enough of men who promised enlightenment while their own lives reeked of ego.

The deeper I went into New Age thought, the more I realized it was unraveling. These teachers—who once seemed so wise, so enlightened—were being exposed for what they really were: charlatans, money-hungry posers, false prophets in saffron robes. Their teachings promised peace, but what I kept finding was more confusion, more noise, more chaos.

Time and perspective became my real teachers. And what I was learning was this: the farther I walked down those roads, the less peace I found.

My mind kept drifting back to where peace had always been—with an invisible cosmic Friend who knew me personally and had shown up in my life when I needed a living, loving companion at my side. That presence had saved me and healed me more times than I could count.

Where would life and circumstances take me next to experience Him—or Her, or Them—again?

Meanwhile, even at the commune, peace was slipping away.

Billy—who fancied himself the next Mick Jagger—and his partner Summer Rain had a room in the basement. Billy set up his amp and microphone down there, and what started as practice quickly became a nightmare. Billy was a tweaker, a full-on speed freak, and when he was wired, he stayed up all night long. Cranking his Fender guitar, screaming into the mic, convinced he was rock and roll's second coming.

When Billy was up, everyone was up. The whole mansion shook. The walls became giant speakers, vibrating with the same three guitar chords played over and over, echoing through the night until sleep was impossible. Billy thought he was brilliant; the rest of us thought he was unbearable.

Leah and I both knew it—we couldn't stay. Not in that house. Not in that chaos. And certainly not with a baby on the way.

And then came the final straw.

The day the Hare Krishna devotees moved in.

One afternoon, I was sitting out front, relaxing on the porch and enjoying the view, when I heard it—cymbals clanging, drums pounding, voices chanting. Down the driveway came a sight so surreal it looked like a scene from a movie.

Seven Hare Krishna devotees, barefoot, heads shaved with a single ponytail dangling, dressed in bright saffron robes, came dancing and twirling up the drive. They beat drums, clashed cymbals, and chanted, "Hare Krishna, Hare Krishna, Hare Rama,

Hare Rama," over and over, their bodies bouncing in rhythm, their voices rising into the humid air.

They stopped at the porch steps. The leader walked right up to me and said they believed Krishna had told them to move in. That it was "God's will."

We let them share a meal, even offered them a room to rest for the night, but they stayed. And stayed. Days turned to weeks, and before long, they were trying to take over the house. Their chanting and clanging filled the air from morning until night, relentless and exhausting. They wanted us to join in, to chant, to dance, to convert.

And then they wanted to run the kitchen. According to their beliefs, food had to be prepared as Prasadam—an offering to Krishna before anyone could eat. The rest of us weren't buying it.

Enough was enough.

We gathered as a household and agreed—they had to go. I told them politely but firmly it was time to leave. They didn't take it well. Their eyes burned with anger. They cursed me, declared I was going against the will of God, and stomped out the same way they came—dancing, chanting, cymbals clanging.

Watching them disappear down the drive was a strange mix of relief and sorrow. But it drove the point home: the dream we were all chasing—the dream of peace, love, communal bliss—it wasn't working.

And it wasn't just the Krishnas.

I'd seen it before in California communes, and now here in Hawaii: the dream always cracked. People wanted Eden. They wanted paradise. They longed to evolve into more enlightened humans, living naturally and organically, in harmony with the world. Noble ideas. But one thing was always missing.

Selflessness.

Without it, every commune was doomed. And in the counterculture world, selflessness was the last thing anyone was interested in. We were all convinced we were gods. "Love the one you're with" was our creed. Do your own thing. Be free. But those very ideas carried destruction in their DNA. The philosophy guaranteed its own failure.

At the heart of it was the belief that if we worked hard enough, fasted long enough, meditated deep enough, purified our diets enough—we could become godlike.

But here's what I had come to see: I wasn't evolving upward. I wasn't becoming godlike. I was collapsing inward.

I had jumped into that whole world with almost no reservations. I had given myself to it fully. But now? I was tired. Weary. Disillusioned.

I began tossing aside the New Age "we are gods" philosophy. I couldn't cling to it anymore. Not when everything in me knew the truth.

I wasn't a god.

I knew I was no god. And if I was, I was a crappy one—lost, confused, and failing miserably.

PART FIVE
THE GOD WHO NEVER LEFT

"I chased peace to Kona, but peace was chasing me. I wasn't the seeker—I was the sought. The Presence was steady, faithful, always there."

CHAPTER TWENTY-ONE
TIME TO GO

By late 1971, the dream was collapsing around me. Communes cracked, gurus failed, and the New Age promises turned to dust. What Leah and I needed now wasn't another philosophy—it was peace. She was pregnant, and the mansion was no place to bring new life. So when old friends invited us to the Kona coast, we packed up and left Hilo behind.

Their names—at least what we all called them—were Cat and Kitten. Their nicknames went back to high school. I'd known them for years.

Cat had been the all-American athlete—football, basketball, baseball. Kitten was the beautiful cheerleader, the popular girl everyone admired. They were the "swells," the golden kids. So when they became hippies, it shocked a lot of people.

After Jeannie and I split up, I lived with them in the Bay Area for a while before they took off for Mexico. They were some of the first of our high school friends to experiment with psychedelics and pot. When they jumped into the counterculture, they went all in. A bunch of our friends followed their lead as they "turned on, tuned in, and dropped out."

They ended up in Puerto Vallarta, where life was cheap and the pot, mushrooms, and peyote were plentiful—until the Mexican authorities arrested them for possession and threw them in jail.

Kitten once told me about her cellmate, a man covered in open sores. He would rub fruit on the wounds before eating it, then offer her a bite. Truly disgusting! It was no wonder that after they were released from jail, they fled out of Mexico as fast as their van could take them.

Still loving the laid-back Mexican lifestyle, they heard the Kona coast had the same climate as Puerto Vallarta—minus the *federales*. The pot was fantastic, coffee shacks were cheap to rent, and the ocean was paradise. They sold their Bay Area house and resettled in Kona.

By then, Leah's old blue van was officially dead. We made the final decision to leave Hilo behind and start over. We gathered our things, said goodbye to the mansion crew, and caught a ride down to Mamalahoa Highway. We stuck out our thumbs and headed for Kona.

Near Waimea, one driver picked us up. As soon as we got in, he turned and asked, "Do you know Jesus?"

That's how we met Nick and Carla—two young hippies bursting to tell how Jesus had saved them. They talked nonstop all the way to Kailua-Kona. I wasn't sure what to make of it, but they were kind, sincere, and likable. Before dropping us off, they told us about their Christian commune, the Pilgrims. As it turned out, that wouldn't be the last time I heard about the Pilgrims.

From Kailua, we caught another ride south down the Kuakini

Highway to the town of Kainaliu, where Cat and Kitten lived on the mountain slopes above the beautiful, blue Pacific Ocean.

We walked down a dirt path to their home, surrounded on both sides by groves of banana trees, papayas, guavas, avocados—even a Chinese lychee nut tree. Cat and Kitten came out of their little coffee shack with their young son, Eric, and greeted us with big hugs. We hadn't seen them in months, and it felt good to be back with friends.

I looked around the property and noticed an old WWII-era four-wheel-drive Army jeep. I'd soon learn that on the Kona coast, four-wheel drive wasn't optional—it was survival. Our place was a small outbuilding on their land—just an old storage shack—but it was home. On the Kona coast, there's a saying: live below the Kuakini Highway and you're *makai* (toward the ocean); above it, you're *mauka* (toward the mountain).

We were *makai*—Mauna Loa at our backs, the Pacific stretched out in front.

The Kona coast was famous for its namesake brew—Kona coffee, one of the most expensive coffees in the world, and there were many coffee plantations along the coast. When a coffee farm stopped producing, the buildings once used to dry and roast beans were often rented out and became homes for the many counterculture hippies. By the early '70s, there were hundreds—maybe even thousands—of hippies living on the Big Island, all chasing the dream of the Age of Aquarius.

Life with Cat and Kitten was good. They shared what they had, made us feel like family, and quickly drew us into their circle of neighbors. Their place had become a meeting place for the local hippie crowd. We often shared meals with neighbors, some of whom had also gone to high school with us in California. One was Jackie Fields, a high school friend of ours, and his wife, Mary.

When Cat's Jeep was running, I'd drive it over to Jackie and Mary's to visit. Mary was young and very pregnant, and Jackie was in the middle of building their house, trying to get it ready in time for the baby. I helped him where I could—hauling materials, wiring things, whatever he needed. Jackie kept insisting he wanted me at the birth. He was set on having a home delivery.

I wasn't too thrilled about that. I was one of the few hippies on the coast to have any medical training. People in the community often came to me with health questions or medical concerns.

Mary wasn't a healthy woman. She had epilepsy and was on Dilantin. She was also diabetic. Not exactly a great candidate for a natural home birth. I tried to explain that, gently, but Jackie wouldn't hear it. He said they were doing it at home, no matter what—even if no one came to help.

To help make ends meet and finance the house project, Jackie had taken a job at the local slaughterhouse—killing steers with a sledgehammer. That was it for most of the hippies. They couldn't handle it. They mainly were strict vegetarians, following a mix of Eastern religions, yoga, karma, and psychedelics. There was no room in their religious philosophy for a 'flesh eating animal murdering fiend.'

I continued to be a friend to Jackie and Mary, visiting them often to offer a helping hand. They were isolated in the community now, pregnant and with few friends, so I decided to be that friend.

I didn't fully understand the weight of that choice until the baby came.

Meanwhile, the wider Kona crowd lived in a wild rhythm of

surfing, spearfishing, *pakalō*, cocaine, mushrooms, opium, and tequila. Free love was the creed, wife-swapping was common, and parties or luaus were constant. Some were still chasing spirituality, but it had a dark edge—witchcraft rituals, peyote visions, sweat lodges, even a fascination with malevolent spirits.

There were still plenty of spiritual seekers and cosmic consciousness types living along the coast—fruitarians meditating and fasting, trying to live off the land—but they didn't run with the ones who hung with Cat and Kitten. I was still a vegetarian, and I wasn't into the drug or party scene. I'd have a little weed or tequila now and then, but I always felt that I didn't fit in with this crowd. Even when I hung with them at times, I felt like an outsider.

My excitement for Eastern religion had burned out. I had gone deeper than most—fasting, celibacy, meditation, raw foods, months in isolation. But union with cosmic consciousness remained a mirage. Every morning, I woke up, and it was still just me. The more I searched, the farther away it seemed. The feeling of union that I was searching for became increasingly a sense of separation.

Every morning, I woke up and I was still there—just me. I found myself becoming cynical, and it was a scary prospect. Nothing terrified me more than losing my sense of wonder at the beauty of creation and my part in it. Nothing I did seemed to bring me closer to what I was looking for—union with the Godhead and with all of creation. I was Don Quixote, jousting at windmills. And yet, I knew for certain there was an invisible world behind the curtain of earthly illusion.

I'd glimpsed something real in moments of clarity: a Presence marked by kindness, compassion, love. Not the selfish love of the counterculture, not the cold, impersonal force of cosmic consciousness. Real love. Other-giving love.

This love is what I was hungry for.

But the Age of Aquarius? It was smoke and mirrors. A counterfeit. A delusion.

So... now what?

All around me, I started noticing more and more Christian converts calling themselves Pilgrims. Hundreds of hippies were leaving the jungles and pouring into Pilgrim houses. It became a running joke—if you so much as hinted at spiritual hunger, someone would ask: "So, are you gonna join the Pilgrims?"

They were everywhere, and I couldn't hitch a ride without hearing another testimony of how Jesus had saved somebody.

I laughed it off. But deep inside, I couldn't help wondering if— maybe—what they'd found was the very thing I'd been chasing all along.

CHAPTER TWENTY-TWO
THE CRADLE AND THE STORM

By mid-January of 1972, Leah was ready to give birth. It had been just over a year since I left the mainland—but it felt like an eternity. So much had happened.

While Leah and I were living on my friend's property, I kept busy building a *koa* wood cradle. Every cut of wood made me more excited for the birth of this child I didn't father but had agreed to stand beside.

When Leah's water broke, we knew it was time. We called Diane, the midwife everyone trusted along the Kona coast, and she came quickly. Leah had been committed to a natural birth from the start—no drugs, no hospitals. That was the way of our community. Birth was supposed to be a sacred event, not a sterile procedure—a kind of party atmosphere, surrounded by friends and family.

But once her contractions began, it didn't feel like a party. Leah was a small woman. She carried a rather large baby. I was concerned this birth would be difficult. She had hours of hard labor ahead of her. I stayed close, rubbing her lower back until my hands cramped, trying to ease the pain she was experiencing.

When she was fully dilated and the baby moved into the birth canal, his head began to crown. The stinging and pain increased— they said it was just pressure, not pain. What B.S. I reminded her to breathe to control the pain and keep her from tearing as the baby came out.

The midwife stayed calm, giving simple instructions. For most of the birth, Leah kept complaining about intense back pain. To help support her, my friend and I got down, slid our arms under her legs, and let her lean on our backs and shoulders. We lifted her off the ground just as the midwife caught the baby. A little boy. Healthy. Whole. Breathing strong.

Within minutes, he was nursing, already at home in the world. Later, I lifted him into the *koa* cradle I had carved, and for the first time, I saw him resting there. Gabriel Philos Rosenburg Land.

It was a holy moment. No drugs. No machines. Just raw life breaking into the world. Not biology alone. Not luck. Not cosmic energy. It was personal. The loving expression of a *being* behind this earthly veil who truly cares for us in a very personal way.

Yet deep inside, I was still mentally experiencing doubt, guilt, fear—and a nagging sense of failure. I couldn't shake it. Even in the wonder of new life, those feelings wouldn't let me rest.

CHAPTER TWENTY-THREE
THE DANCE OF THE GODS

A few months after moving to the Kona coast, we were at one of the usual get-togethers at Cat's house when we met a middle-aged man named Lonnie. He was a short, plump fellow with long blond hair down to his shoulders—but very bald on top. He really was a comical-looking character. Lonnie was an ocean-going sea captain, a caricature of what you might imagine a sea captain to be. Loud, full of wild stories—bragging about his conquests with women, and his bravery in brawls and gunfights. But I always thought he was a better person than he tried to project.

Lonnie had just bought sixteen acres of property in Honaunau, one of the oldest farms on the Kona coast. At the turn of the century, it had been a successful Japanese coffee, banana, avocado, and macadamia nut farm, but now it was overgrown and falling apart. Lonnie captained a ship that pulled barges across the ocean, so he was gone for half the year and wanted a place to live when he was home. The farm needed serious work. I was an experienced gardener and a hard worker, and as we talked, it seemed like a perfect fit. He invited me to come over and see what we could do together.

At the same time, Leah wanted to go back to California to show Gabriel to her parents. Her family sent her enough money for the trip, so she left for a couple of months.

After meeting with Lonnie, we agreed that I could move onto the farm, and a portion of the land would be mine to cultivate as I saw fit. My labor would cover the rent. There were two houses on the property and a large coffee drying floor with a roll-on roll-off roof. I said goodbye to Cat and Kitten, packed our few possessions, thanked them for everything they'd done for us, and moved to "Lila" Farm. In Hindu culture, *līlā* means the dance of the gods—or the cosmic joke. Turned out to be prophetic.

The drying floor was built on a steep slope, raised on supports. Underneath it was a storage room with a coffee roasting machine (which we never used) and enough space for me to live in while I worked. I began the big job of raising that heavy roof using a car jack—inch by inch, day after day—propping it up with 55-gallon barrels as I went. Eventually, I got it eight feet off the ground. Then I hiked into the *ohia* forest above the farm, harvested ten logs using a friend's chainsaw, and set them as permanent supports. Thankfully, my friend Cal helped me cut and haul those heavy *ohia* logs. That wood was as hard as oak—a perfect building material.

The new house turned out beautifully. I built a balcony on the back where I could look out over the coastline—maybe fifty miles of the Pacific. We were at about 1,700 feet elevation, *mauka* of the highway, and almost directly above the City of Refuge. I could see Kealakekua Bay—Captain Cook Bay. It was the perfect elevation:

not too hot or cold, with just the right amount of rain for farming. I lived there for most of 1972 until May of 1974.

Lonnie and I worked hard to get the farm back in shape. We started with the bananas, hauling organic fertilizer—coffee bean husks—from the Captain Cook Kona Coffee Company. Acres of husks had been composting in the sun for years. We shoveled them into a pickup, drove them into the groves, and shoveled them back out again. We hauled tons of compost that year.

By the end of the year, we were harvesting banana bunches that had been maturing for two years—some weighing 200 pounds. We cut them from the stalks, broke them into hands, and boxed them for shipping to Alaska and Canada. We'd joined a *huey*—a collective of local farmers who worked together to sell and ship their produce.

We also cultivated avocados. Some of ours were massive—three or four pounds each. Even in 1972, we were getting twenty-five cents apiece. We harvested thousands of pounds in '72 and '73, selling through our Honaunau cooperative, mostly made up of Filipino and Hawaiian farmers. One of those farmers was Brother Profurio, a local Filipino pastor at an Assembly of God church in Kona. He and I became good friends—though I had no idea how important he'd later become in my life.

My own piece of the property—about two acres, part of the agreement with Lonnie—was breathtakingly beautiful. I would stand on my balcony, look down on that land, and feel an overwhelming sense of gratitude and thankfulness to the One who seemed to care for me so deeply.

But the land needed work. The *hanohano* grass—a fast-growing vine that could grow almost a foot a day—had taken over everything. I cleared it by hand in the intense heat. Once the brush was gone, I began building lava rock walls to terrace the hillside for vegetable beds. I couldn't wait to start growing organic vegetables to sell at the local markets.

We also started growing *pakalolo*—marijuana—on the upper acreage. I didn't sell it, but my partner Jeff did. I sometimes traded for building materials, but never for money. The weed was worth a fortune and became famous. Some big-name rock stars were smoking the pot Jeff and I grew and offering huge sums for it. Jeff made money off it. I didn't. It became a sore spot between us.

Leah and Gabriel eventually came back and moved into the new coffee shack I had built. I loved spending time with Gabriel. He was just a few months old, but I'd take him down to the beach, get him wet, and play in the waves. He laughed at everything— such a good-natured little guy. I loved rocking with him in the hammock, his little chest on mine. He was really smart and seemed to be advanced for his age.

But with Leah, it wasn't that much fun. Naturally, she wanted to settle down. She wanted marriage. I couldn't do it. I wasn't in love with her, and marriage was never part of the arrangement when I stepped in to help her through the pregnancy. To me, we were just good friends. That was all. Marriage was out of the question. But it left us in an impossible situation.

Leah knew she had some hard decisions to make—for herself and for Gabriel. One day she told me she was thinking about becoming a Pilgrim and moving into one of their communal houses. I was shocked that she was even considering this move. I did everything I could to talk her out of it.

In the end, she chose to go back to the mainland instead.

CHAPTER TWENTY-FOUR

THE CALM BEFORE THE BREAK

Life on Lila Farm came with a gift—I could finally surf again. My favorite break was down at Keei, a shallow reef in a Filipino fishing village almost directly below the farm.

It was the perfect situation for a surfer. If the waves were up in the afternoon, I'd work the farm in the morning—mostly shoveling and spreading fertilizer on the bananas and avocados and tending my organic garden.

This amazing lifestyle—being so close to the ocean and the land—was incredible. The wonders of nature caused me to drink deeply and be aware of the love of God all around me, and the connection I knew that I had on the inside and outside.

Out in the water one day, I met a young married couple who loved to surf my favorite point break. We became fast friends. Calvin and Claire were incredible water people. Claire was a lovely, brown-skinned Tahitian-Hawaiian woman, and Cal was a blond, blue-eyed guy from the East Coast who'd transplanted himself to Kona. Claire was a women's surfing champion from

Oahu—graceful and powerful in the ocean. She swam like a dolphin, moved like the water was part of her, and could stay underwater longer than anyone I'd ever known.

Cal worked on a local cattle ranch, tending cows from horseback. He was a fabulous horseman. The Kona coast had some enormous ranches, and gathering cattle or fixing fences through rocky volcanic forests and wide meadows was tough, never-ending work.

The three of us surfed and spearfished together whenever we could. Cal helped me on the farm when he had time, and eventually we went in together on an outrigger canoe and some fishing nets. We'd paddle out into the ocean, dive down, and set our nets in spots we knew would yield fish.

Diving along the Kona coast was the kind of experience you never forget. As we dove down to set our nets, barracuda, big blue *uhu*, moray eels, and myriads of brilliantly colored reef fish would cruise past—sometimes even a shark. We were diving along the side of the tallest mountain on earth, and the descent was unreal. At first, the sunlit coral and rock were clearly visible, but then the ocean would shift—growing darker and deeper until all you could see was endless, black-blue water. The drop-off was dramatic. The sea just disappeared into tens of thousands of feet of depth.

It was eerie. Almost frightening. I'd look down into that deep, mysterious blue and imagine some giant shark emerging from the abyss. It was never totally peaceful—always a hint of the unknown. Seeing a shark cruise by near the reef was actually easier to handle than wondering what might be down there, just out of sight.

The area we fished had underwater channels that stretched all the way to the cliffs above the surf. We'd wait for the ocean surge to rush through, set our nets, and then as the surge receded, fish would be washed right into them. The rugged channels were breathtaking. Rocks covered in bright seaweed and coral, swaying like dancers in the push and pull of the tide. Schools of iridescent reef fish darted in and out, flashing in the shifting light.

It was mesmerizing. Addictive.

We were diving about 15 to 20 feet underwater—no diving equipment—just a mask, snorkel, fins, and a knife. When we pulled up our nets, they were usually loaded with fish—and sometimes octopus. We'd eat the octopus raw as soon as we got out of the ocean. It was a delicious treat, especially with the fresh seaweed we harvested off the rocks. We supplemented our diet with those fish, octopus, and ʻopihi—shellfish we'd pry off the rocks.

The ocean held mysteries I never expected—wonders and terrors you can't grasp until you're face-to-face with them.

One day, I was diving and poking around underwater caves, looking for lobsters. Kona lobsters get huge—and they're delicious. I spotted one cave and decided to investigate. I was about 15 feet down. As I swam up to the opening and peered into the dark, something started coming out toward me.

It was a gigantic moray eel.

I had no idea they could get that big. Its head bumped my face-mask. I froze, terrified to move. The thing kept coming—its mouth wide enough to bite me in half. Its body kept turning, unwinding, until the whole thing was out of the cave.

It was thicker than I was, and at least 12 feet long. It slowly turned and glided away without a sound.

I was out of air and shot up to the surface as fast as I could. I'll never forget that moment. It was shocking. Terrifying. That eel should've ended me. But once again, my invisible Friend was there, saving me.

We kept our outrigger canoe down at the beach by the City of Refuge, an ancient Hawaiian site with thousand-year-old stone walls, reconstructed houses, and wooden idols once worshipped by their people. Local wood carvers worked there, shaping traditional canoes from massive single logs just like their ancestors had done centuries before. It was a magical place. In those days, if a criminal or anyone who had broken *kapu*—the sacred law—could reach the City of Refuge, he was safe. Forgiven. Free from death or punishment.

The times I spent fishing, surfing, and diving with Cal and Claire were truly times of refuge and rest. But that rest wasn't going to last long. Spiritually, I was being pulled fast toward a destination I couldn't control.

It felt like my life was balanced on the crest of a gigantic wave —one that was about to break and shatter every philosophy and idea I thought I knew about reality. My cosmic glue philosophy had already started coming unglued before I ever left the mainland.

I had no idea how much crow I was about to eat.

CHAPTER TWENTY-FIVE

THE HYPOCRISY AND THE HUNGER

I had a friend who lived up above Lila Farm who was a professional pot farmer. One day, he came down upset, saying he'd heard the Pilgrims were praying for his pot plants to die. And the weird thing was—they were. For no reason anyone could explain, the plants were shriveling up.

If that was true, it struck me as pure hypocrisy. So I decided to find out for myself.

The Pilgrims seemed to be taking over the Kona coast—Manna Trading Company, the Canaan Deli, Fishsticks surfboard shop. All run as Christian businesses. I sold my lettuce, squash, and spinach to Manna, and I'll admit they did a lot of good. The Fellowship itself was exploding with roughly thirty communal houses, a five-acre organic farm, and over three hundred people showing up at their meetings.

I heard they held prayer meetings at the Manna in the evenings, open to anyone. So one night I went.

They welcomed me—coffee, pastries, smiles. Then the prayers

began. One man sat in the corner, praying in a strange tongue. The rest of us, maybe twenty-five, sat cross-legged in a circle.

Names were called out across Kona. Then they got to Brent. "Lord, save his soul," they prayed—then turned to cursing the "evil spirit of marijuana," demanding his plants shrivel and die. "We curse you, Satan! Release Brent from bondage!"

That was it. I stood up, furious. "You creeps! How dare you pray for Brent's pot to die? He worked hard for that crop. You're a bunch of hypocrites. If this is Christianity, I want nothing to do with it—or with you." And I stormed out.

The Pilgrims were everywhere. Hitchhiking was my usual way of getting around, and half the time they were the ones picking me up. Which meant I'd get their testimonies, whether I wanted them or not. Some were kind, gentle, and genuine. But not all of them. Others called me wicked and told me I was headed straight to the devil's hell unless I accepted Jesus as my Lord and Savior.

As a spiritual seeker, I felt above the whole thing—more "advanced" than people pushing a bloody Jesus on a cross.

And then, Brent—the same friend whose pot plants were dying—joined the Pilgrims. I couldn't believe it.

Still, not all my encounters with them were bad. At the Manna Trading Company, one young woman stood out. Paula Goulding.

She worked the register, and we often talked about faith. She never pressured, never condemned. She was kind. Gentle. Different. One day I walked in with a load of produce, and she was behind the counter playing guitar, singing about the mercies of God.

As she sang, something stirred deep in me. Peace. Love. The kind I couldn't fake or argue away. It wasn't judgment. It wasn't wrath. It was real.

If what I saw in her eyes was true Christianity, I wanted it. I'll never forget Paula.

Footnote: Paula Goulding. Years later, the Pilgrims fell apart, and Paula was deeply wounded. She divorced, moved to Alaska, and in 1983 was abducted and murdered by the serial killer known as the Butcher Baker. A film was made about the case. Paula was the best Christian I ever knew. Today, I believe she's safe—singing in the arms of the Lover of her soul.

Lila Farm had become a magnet for well-known musicians and actors. Often, they would anchor their sailing ships down below us in Kealakekua Bay, and their crews would come up to join the partying and luaus at the farm. Teddy, who had a house on the farm with us, would supply them with the best pot in the Hawaiian islands.

For my taste, there were too many people dabbling in hard drugs—cocaine, speed, heroin.

The parties at Lila Farms weren't just about the drugs, though. They were also filled with music, food, and friends gathering under the stars. Like anywhere in those days, there were people chasing women, drugs, and noise, but for most of us, it was simply life on a working farm. Lonnie married, and a giant named Stretch moved in—6'7", a natural charmer, always surrounded by newcomers fresh off the plane. Jeff, who lived above me, was popular too, though he was into heroin. I hated it. We bodysurfed together sometimes, but drugs drove a wedge between us. And when I spoke up, no one wanted to hear my complaints. I withdrew more—surfing, fishing, farming. That was my world.

By then, I'd dropped strict vegetarianism—fish, eggs, cheese. I no longer believed groceries could bring God-consciousness. Most of my New Age philosophy was gone; the hypocrisy rattled me.

What remained was a casual dependence on the I Ching, the Urantia Book, and a few Hawaiian superstitions. I didn't make major decisions without throwing the I Ching. Urantia fascinated me—2,000 pages on onion-skin paper, supposedly from celestial beings. It called Jesus the savior of our galaxy, denied blood sacrifice, and said other galaxies had their own "saviors." At the time, it felt more believable than the hell-preaching I kept hearing. Looking back, it was closer to Mormonism than truth.

Even so, I'd slipped into a kind of hopeless cynicism. On paper, I was living the dream—tropical farm, ocean, freedom—but joy was gone. I only felt alive underwater, hunting fish along the reef. Those were the moments I felt closest to what I then called "Deity."

And yet I found myself leaning toward Jesus—not from doctrine, but because in some Christians I saw an authentic love missing from my New Age friends. Not all of them—just some. But that difference mattered. It wouldn't leave me alone—and it was about to follow me home.

CHAPTER TWENTY-SIX

THINGS FALL APART

Leah and Gabriel had been gone for months, and I missed them. I was living a lonely life—even with all the people constantly coming and going from Lila Farm. There were plenty of beautiful women in Honaunau. Several times, I tried to start a relationship with some of the organic mamas around Kona, but nothing ever clicked. I kept finding myself alone.

Out of that frustration—and a generally bad attitude—I found myself getting more and more irritated with many of the Pilgrims that I was constantly meeting. It seemed they were *everywhere*, from one end of the Kona coast to the other. And I was so tired of hearing all the same testimonies, cut from the same mold: how they got 'saved,' how miserable they used to be, and how Jesus had rescued them.

Then, with the same breath, they'd say Jesus loved me and I was the apple of His eye.

It was such a schizophrenic message. It made no sense.

I'd had enough. If I saw a Pilgrim hitchhiking—even in the pouring rain—I'd drive right past, smile, and wave, leaving them standing there. I was that done.

One Saturday night (I'd started drinking a bit too much by then), I had way too much tequila. I drove past their meeting place —Saturday was their big gathering night—and I tossed an empty booze bottle right at the front door. Strange how things turn out. My story with the Pilgrims only got weirder later—but that's for another time

Their meeting place was called the Pilgrim's Inn. Before the Christians took it over, it was a whorehouse motel known as the Kona Nightingale—named after the wild donkeys that brayed along the Kona coast. When the Pilgrims moved in, they turned it into a communal house. Brothers lived on one side, sisters on the other, and in the middle was a big lobby that doubled as a meeting hall, with a commercial kitchen tucked behind it.

Several nights a week the place shook with loud music, fiery preaching, and noisy celebrations of their "salvation." They opened the doors wide—meals, showers, and beds for the stream of hippie travelers drifting through. And plenty of them never left. They became Pilgrims.

To me, that was troubling. These were the same seekers I'd known in the jungles and mountains, people who had tried everything but Jesus. Now, by the hundreds, they were flocking to this movement. It shocked me. Honestly, it put a giant question mark in the middle of everything I thought I knew about truth.

Most of these people had been just like me—spiritual seekers who'd tried everything *but* Jesus. To see them abandon the jungles and mountains and flock to Christianity by the hundreds was shocking.

Absolutely mind-blowing.

And it planted a giant question mark in the middle of all my ideas about truth.

I didn't realize it at the time, but spiritually, I was just steps away from becoming completely undone.

My tropical paradise was rapidly becoming something else—definitely not a paradise. Trouble was brewing all along the Kona Coast. Drug use among locals and hippies was exploding, and with that came demand for heroin, meth, black tar opium, and more. Prices were sky-high, and organized crime started showing up to take a cut. Hawaiian, Filipino, and Chinese gangs moved in, often using local hoodlums to do their dirty work.

It wasn't just pot and psychedelics anymore. This was big money—and the gangs wanted control, even if they had to steal it. We began hearing stories of home invasions and brutal beatings. The dream of paradise was slipping fast into chaos. Organized gangs were moving in, and a lot of us suspected even some in authority were turning a blind eye—or worse.

Looking back over those years—from 1968 to 1974—I realized I had tried just about every spiritual path. Psychedelic mushrooms, LSD, peyote, mescaline. Hindu gurus. Buddhism. Vegetarianism (and let me tell you, you can't find God in your groceries). Transcendental Meditation. Solitude in the wilderness. Fasting.

And all of it had left me more cynical than before.

What was I even searching for?

Why had I thrown myself so fully into these disciplines that promised spiritual awakening—yet left me emptier than when I started? Could it be that my friends who had become Christians had actually found the truth? Was it possible that the thing I'd spent my life seeking had been right there all along?

I was starting to ask deeper questions. I was looking for the one behind the curtain—the person behind the scenes of my life. The one who kept showing up. The one who kept saving me. Whoever they were... I knew this much: They cared for me. They had their hand on me.

What was going on really hit home for me in early 1973.

I'd been sitting on the stone sea wall beside beautiful Kailua Bay with some friends, enjoying a cold beer on a hot day. My friend Bob was there with a visiting family from California—a mom, a dad, and their baby. They were wide-eyed with excitement to be vacationing in paradise. They were staying with Bob, who lived just up the hill from me.

What I didn't know at the time was that Bob had been selling a lot of drugs out of his house—including heroin. Apparently, there was a lot of money flowing through that operation.

A few days later, I was home on the farm, relaxing under the shade of a macadamia nut tree, when a friend pulled up the long driveway to my place. The moment he got out of the car, I could see something was seriously wrong.

He was shaken.

I asked what had happened, and with a broken look in his eyes, he told me Bob and the entire visiting family had been murdered. The only survivor was the baby.

I was stunned. Shocked. I had just been with them a few days before. The news didn't seem real.

It was a home invasion, he said—an organized gang. They'd come for the money and the drugs. And they'd left nothing but horror behind.

The way they'd killed them was so violent, so gruesome, it made me physically ill. They'd used machetes and an axe. Their bodies had been dismembered and scattered throughout the house, while the baby lay alone in its bassinet.

The names of a couple of local gang leaders were being whispered—everyone on the Kona coast seemed to know who they were. In the hippie community, it was just accepted that these guys were behind the murders. They were known for intimidation, and people believed they'd killed before. But nothing ever stuck. No one dared to testify against them.

They were trying to control the drug trade in Hawaii—and using murder and fear to do it.

This entire scene was beyond anything I could comprehend. I was just a hippie-dippy farmer and surfer. I had nothing to do with that level of darkness. But now it was on my doorstep, and I couldn't unsee it.

Our idyllic dream of paradise on the Kona coast was unraveling fast. Fear was gripping everyone. The innocence and freedom we'd once felt were being drowned by violence and paranoia.

The whole world felt like it was falling apart.

The next few weeks were hard as so many of us tried to process what had just happened. There was no understanding of the level of greed and evil that had been unleashed. This wasn't the world I came searching for when I moved to the Big Island. I came looking for God and peace—nonviolence and love.

The Age of Aquarius we'd all hoped for was dissolving... fading into some distant, unreachable dream.

And yet—the God or being who'd protected me from death

and disaster time after time wasn't finished with me. Once again, He showed up. And through another rescue, He would finally reveal His true identity.

CHAPTER TWENTY-SEVEN
A GOD WHO WEEPS

After Gabriel's birth, I got to know the local midwife pretty well. Once I moved to Lila Farm, I had the opportunity to help her with some of the natural childbirths along the coast. Even though Gabriel and Leah had returned to California, his birth had left an indelible impression on me. I could see the hand of God in it—see His great love for us humans.

I knew the One who had been close to me all along—the One who loved me and protected me—was real. Even though invisible, this presence was unmistakable. And I had come to believe that this being wasn't just there for me, but for everyone... if only we paid attention.

This presence wasn't some impersonal New Age 'Christ consciousness' or vague spiritual force we all used to talk about. No, this being was personal. I knew Him that way even as a boy— interested in my every thought, soothing every pain and wound, both physical and emotional. Somehow, I had come full circle—

arriving back where I began—in the simplicity of a God of love, the one I had first encountered in childhood.

As I've said before, I was the only hippie around with any real medical knowledge, so people felt secure when I was nearby for emergencies. I ended up assisting at several births, and I felt comfortable doing it. There's something almost sacred about witnessing new life enter this world and then watching those little ones grow. I was infatuated with the wonder of it all.

Most of the births in our counterculture community were uneventful and beautiful. These brave mamas were committed to delivering naturally, outside of sterile hospital rooms, without drugs or anesthesia. And what a gift it was for the dads—to be there, to hold their babies first, not some stranger in scrubs. Mom's got to nurse right away. Babies got to feel the heartbeat of their mothers. It was raw and real and deeply human.

But not every natural birth ends with joy. Not every story ends with celebration.

What came next was one of the saddest—and most life-changing—experiences of my life.

Life on Lila Farm had become something I tried to escape from as often as I could. I still loved my veggie gardens, tending the avocado trees, and caring for the banana groves—but the endless parties and steady flow of drugs were wearing me down. The beautiful Kona coast, with all of its wonder, became my sanctuary. It was the perfect place to get away from what felt like a rapidly deteriorating scene.

I had decided to go hiking and do some cliff climbing at the City of Refuge—like I've mentioned before, it was located on the coast, about 1,800 feet below Lila Farm. It was also where Calvin and I kept our outrigger canoe.

That same week, my friend Jackie—you might remember him, the guy who worked at the slaughterhouse—and his wife Mary, were due to deliver their baby. They lived in Kainaliu, and I had real concerns about Mary having a home birth. I'd said before, I didn't think natural childbirth without a doctor or hospital was a good idea for her. Mary had multiple serious health issues— epilepsy for one—and was on Dilantin for seizures along with other medications. But Jackie was determined. He was set on doing this at home, no matter what anyone else thought.

I made the trip down to the City of Refuge and hiked the mile or so until I reached the high cliffs I intended to scale. The trail leading there was over a thousand years old—used by the ancient Hawaiians as they traveled the coastline on extended fishing expeditions. It was paved with stones they'd placed by hand, hundreds of years before, and each day's journey would end at a sleeping cave or a fishing camp.

I loved walking where the ancients had walked. The area was thick with a forest of spiny *keawe* trees and the occasional coconut palm. Rugged. Remote. Hot.

Sometimes I'd head out for days, sleeping in the caves and spear fishing in the ocean that bordered the trail. Now and then, I came across remnants of abandoned Hawaiian villages, left just as they were centuries ago. It was one of the driest parts of the island, almost desert-like, with very little rain.

I often explored the lava tube caves that wound deep through the earth in a maze of narrow passageways. Some went on for miles. I'd find small pools of water in the darkness, filled with tiny red shrimp that had adapted to life with no light.

But today, I wasn't hiking—I was planning to scale the high black lava cliffs that rose above the *pāhoehoe* lava and the *keawe* forest. The cliffs had multiple plateaus, each one leading higher to a network of caves formed by ancient eruptions.

I'd climbed them many times before, checking out the caves. On one trip, I entered a large lava tube that stretched for 50 or 60 feet and was lined down the center with wooden shelving. Both sides were stacked with cardboard boxes, each one labeled by archaeologists. Inside were skulls and bones—human remains collected from the caves along the coast.

It felt wrong. Disrespectful. I had no idea why they would collect and store the bones that way. These were the resting places of the ancient Hawaiians. It didn't sit well with me.

This time, I was climbing a near-vertical face, reaching up to find a handhold. As I pulled myself toward the next ledge, I noticed a pile of bones—rats, mongooses, maybe a few birds.

Then, just as my fingers hooked the edge, the silence shattered. Three giant white owls burst from the nest and dive-bombed me, wings thrashing the air. Their talons and beaks came so close to my eyes I was sure I'd be blinded. I was terrified. I thought I might lose my grip and fall backward off the 40-foot cliff.

Somehow—miraculously—I made it back down the cliff with some scratches and a new respect for those giant owls.

I had mentioned before that I'd developed a real interest in Hawaiian superstitions and legends—especially because I spent so much time canoeing, spearfishing, and exploring the ancient coastline. I felt a deep connection to the old ways and the people who came before us. There was something sacred about walking the same trails, diving in the same waters, and sleeping in the same caves.

As I thought about what had just happened—being attacked

by those white owls in broad daylight—one particular legend came rushing back to me.

The Hawaiians believed that if you saw a white owl during the day, it was an omen. A warning. A sign that death was coming.

At the time, it seemed like a strange belief. But I'd come to learn that the Hawaiians were often right in their superstitions.

As I got into my car, I noticed another vehicle coming up fast—way too fast for that rough road. It pulled up beside me and a friend from the farm jumped out, clearly frantic.

"John, there is an emergency. You've got to come right now—Mary's in labor, and Jackie wants you there for the birth. Now!"

The strange thing is, I hadn't told a soul where I was going. The City of Refuge is remote, and the road leading down to where I was isn't exactly easy to find. To this day, I have no idea how they located me.

I believe my invisible friend—the one who never seemed to leave me—was guiding me to help my friends through the most terrible and painful experience of their lives.

I jumped in the car, and we sped away down the rough dirt road until we reached the highway and headed south toward Kainaliu, where Jackie and Mary lived. When we arrived, the midwife was already there. Someone had picked her up too. Remember, there were no telephones or electricity in many of these houses—we were isolated, down a dirt road, miles from civilization.

I went into the house and into Mary's bedroom, where I found Jackie, the midwife, and Mary already deeply in labor. The baby was in the birth canal. What I saw terrified me. Mary was in terrible pain, having the worst back labor I had ever witnessed. The baby was stuck. The midwife and I had arrived too late.

Jackie and Mary had refused to go to the hospital, so there had been no way to monitor whether the baby was in distress or in the wrong position. Mary couldn't stop pushing. She was crying, straining—completely overwhelmed.

As the midwife and I knelt to help her, we were met with something neither of us had ever encountered. The baby was in a rare and dangerous breech position—his body twisted in a way that made the delivery almost impossible. We could see immediately that something was terribly wrong. It was too late for a hospital, too late for a cesarean. All we could do now was try to help Mary and do our best to deliver the child.

We did everything we could, but he was already gone. When we finally delivered him, it was clear he had died some time before.

Mary sobbed, pleading to hold her baby. We were holding her dead infant in our hands. The pain of knowing we had to tell her— it was more than I thought I could bear. We gently laid the child on her chest. She held him against her heart for a long time, maybe hoping it wasn't real—that it was some awful mistake and he might start breathing after all.

Jackie came to her side, broken and weeping. He lifted his son into his arms and kissed him.

As I stood beside the midwife—devastated and helpless— something cracked open inside me. I understood in that moment just how precious a single human life is. And I sensed, more deeply than ever, that there is a God in heaven who cares for us. Who weeps with us. Who enters our grief.

Maybe those hippie friends who had become "Pilgrims" were right. Maybe there *is* a Father who loves us—one who isn't far off, but with us.

I longed to hold Mary and Jackie in my arms, to comfort them, to tell them they were not alone. That there was Someone who saw them. Loved them. And would help them through this tragedy.

If only I had known then what I know now.

After his son's death, Jackie lovingly carved a small *koa* wood casket. We buried the child on a hillside overlooking the Kona Coast and the endless blue of the Pacific Ocean.

My heart was shattered, carrying their pain and devastation. I knew I had to discover who this being was—the one who had so often invaded my life. I wanted to be able to tell everyone: He's real. He's there. You are never alone. Never unloved.

I didn't know it then, but the God who weeps with us was about to reveal Himself.

The God who had never left me—not once, not ever.

PART SIX
ALL SHALL BE WELL

"Love had never left—I just hadn't recognized His face."

All along, the God who never left was quietly weaving His way through my chaos.

Through the danger, the heartbreak, the searching, He had been there.

But now something was shifting. It wasn't just His presence anymore — it was His identity breaking through.

I didn't know it yet, but I was about to discover the truth that would undo all my striving, silence all my fears, and finally bring me peace: Love Himself had been with me all along — Father, Son, and Spirit, closer than my breath.

This last section of my story is about that awakening — how the invisible Friend I had been aware of for so long revealed Himself in Jesus, and how His love changed everything.

CHAPTER TWENTY-EIGHT

The Bible, the Blues, and a Backslidden Christian

I was driving down the Kuakini Highway, heading back from the grocery store, when I spotted a big blond guy hitchhiking. I pulled over. He was a giant, soft-spoken Greek with a quick smile.

"Paul Papoulias," he said as he climbed in.

The first thing out of his mouth was, "Do you have any pot?"

I laughed and said I did. Right away, I liked him. Some people you just know you'll click with from the very first conversation. Paul was one of them.

Looking back, I'd call it a divine appointment. My invisible Friend—the one who'd been quietly shadowing me all along—was behind this meeting. I didn't know it then, but I was being led toward the answer to my greatest question: *Who are You?*

I took Paul up to the farm and handed him a small bag of pot—nothing special, mostly leaves. As I've said before, even though I grew it, I rarely smoked it myself. And I never turned it into a business. A little bartering here and there for supplies, sure—but money was never what I was after.

Paul surprised me. "John, I'm a backslidden Christian. I shouldn't even be smoking this. But thank you for being generous. I want to give you something far more valuable."

He reached into his pack and pulled out a well-worn Bible— creases in the pages, the cover soft with use. He handed it to me with both hands, like it was a treasure.

Turns out Paul was a musician—a guitar player. After that first meeting, we saw each other often. He gave me a guitar and came up to the farm for lessons. We laughed, played, and made music. Sometimes he brought along an old bluesman named Willie, who poured out songs from another era. Sitting around listening to them play was medicine for the soul.

Paul's wife, Maria, was a petite, dark-haired Mexican woman. The three of us became good friends. God knows I needed that.

The thing about Paul that stood out above everything else was his love for Jesus. It wasn't religion. It wasn't preachy. It was real. And that Bible he gave me? I had no idea it would change the entire course of my life.

But outside those nights of music and laughter, the world around me was unraveling fast. By then, I was growing more and more disenchanted with the hippie movement. Not the lifestyle itself—there was still something beautiful in our connection to the land and the rhythm of nature—but the culture was shifting. Selfishness was replacing love, betrayal replacing trust. The most admired people weren't those with wisdom or heart—they were the ones with the best dope or the prettiest wives. People sat in circles smoking pot or snorting coke, drifting off into their own heads. It wasn't fellowship—just a roomful of people lost in their own trips.

The sexual looseness soured me even more. And truthfully, I was a hypocrite in judging it—I had been guilty myself. But the pain my unfaithfulness had caused my ex-wife and child had seared something into me. I couldn't unsee the destruction it left behind.

Eventually, it hit home. The disregard I'd been observing wasn't just out there—it was in my own house. I found out that some of my so-called friends had been sleeping with Leah behind my back. That betrayal cut deeper than I expected.

What had once seemed like a free and loving lifestyle was collapsing into suspicion and betrayal, all wrapped in a counterfeit version of love. When violence started creeping into the Kona community, I knew I was getting close to being done with it all.

CHAPTER TWENTY-NINE
THE FARM, THE FAME, AND THE FALL

In the weeks after Jackie and Mary's loss, I found myself questioning everything more deeply—what mattered, what was real, what I could still believe in. But the world around me didn't stop. If anything, things were accelerating—and not in a good way.

By now, Teddy was becoming famous for supplying *pakalolo* to rock stars and the rich and famous. He made regular trips to Maui to deliver his product, and his name was known far beyond the islands—not just by musicians, but by people who operated in much darker corners. The word was that organized crime had started paying attention. Eventually, he built his dream house on Lila Farm, just down the slope from my coffee shack, separated only by a grove of bananas and a field of coffee trees.

I liked him, his wife Vivian, and their little boy, Moonie. There was a strange rumor going around—that Vivian had been "given" to Teddy as a gift from a friend. Supposedly, she stayed with him not as a slave, but willingly. However, she wasn't a very happy person. She always looked a little sad, like the joy had drained out of her. Still, she loved Moonie with her whole heart. She cared for him tenderly and doted on him constantly.

I often worked for Teddy, helping with building projects on his house. So I was down the hill from my place a lot, working on his property.

The hippies out in the Puna district near Hilo were starting to rake in serious money—same with the counterculture crowd along the Kona coast. It was a recipe for disaster. That kind of cash was bound to attract the wrong type of attention. Jeff, who lived just up the hill from me on Lila Farm, was selling high-grade weed and cruising around in a brand-new Toyota Land Cruiser. That alone was like putting up a billboard for the mob: There's money here. Come and get it.

Me? I was still just a hippie-dippy. I had no interest in making money. I was happy with my garden, tending the bananas and avocado trees, surfing, diving, fishing—just living close to the earth and enjoying God's creation.

The rest of the story is almost unbelievable—but every word of it is true. I didn't choose to get mixed up in the dope scene; it pulled me in. Living on Lila Farm meant I was caught in its undertow. I had poured my life into that land and couldn't just walk away. So I stayed, even as things spiraled. But deep down in my soul, I could feel it—something was drawing me in. Something that promised to satisfy every longing I'd ever carried... to know the truth about everything, including who I really was.

As I've written before, Lila Farm sat on the slope of Mauna Loa like a natural amphitheater. Sound carried with eerie clarity—you could hear neighbors from almost anywhere on the hillside.

All the houses on the farm—scattered across the hillside—could hear each other without much effort. From the veranda of my coffee shack, I often could hear Teddy and his wife talking, laughing, or entertaining guests down below. Remember, his house was just one coffee field and a banana grove beneath mine.

I still called it a shack, but over time, I had turned it into a real home. It had become a beautiful house with a million-dollar view of the Kona coast and the endless stretch of Pacific Ocean. But the sounds of life echoed clearly across the hill—from farmhouses, from neighbors, and from one place in particular...

There was a Filipino dance hall down the road. Because very few Filipino women had been brought to Hawaii to work the plantations, the dance hall became a community hub for Filipino men. Hippie girls would get paid 50 cents to dance with the men who came, and for a bit more, the men were allowed a feel or a pinch while dancing. The music pounded late into the night, the booze flowed freely, and the noise was impossible to ignore.

Why do I mention this? Its significance will become clear soon enough.

But first, I want to explain why I keep emphasizing the acoustics of this hillside. Without understanding just how clearly sound carried across Lila Farm, the story I'm about to tell might seem impossible to believe.

After I met Paul Papoulias and he gave me his Bible, I started reading it almost every night. I'd usually pour a little wine and maybe take a single hit off a joint—though I rarely smoked weed anymore—then sit down and read. I didn't understand much of it, but the Gospels... they spoke to me.

By the end of 1973, most of my old spiritual books had been shelved. Only the Bible remained on my table. As I've shared before, I was still tossing the ancient Chinese I Ching for answers —seeking clarity about different questions in life. One night, almost as a joke, I asked whether I should keep the I Ching or the Bible. In its usual cryptic way, the I Ching told me to keep the Bible.

Looking back, that moment would make Paul's gift of the Bible feel strangely prophetic.

CHAPTER THIRTY

WHEN DARKNESS FELL

Toward the end of 1973—some of the timelines blur a little, but I'll do my best to piece it together—I was jolted awake around midnight by the sound of blood-curdling screams and gunshots echoing from the house just below mine.

It was coming from Teddy's place, a close friend and neighbor on Lila Farm. I had worked for Teddy doing various jobs, including helping him build this very house. Teddy was well known for growing *pakalōlo* on the island, and the money it brought in made him a perfect target for thieves. So when I heard the noise and screaming I was immediately awake and knew he was being robbed.

My whole body broke out in goosebumps. My heart slammed against my chest. Then I heard it—Vivian's voice, frantic and pleading:

"Please, Lowell—don't kill my baby!"

More screaming. Heavy blows. And then my neighbor's voice

—struggling, gasping. You could tell from the sound alone: something brutal was happening.

When I heard Lowell's name screamed

I knew.

Something unspeakable was going down.

Everyone in Kona had whispered about him before—rumors of earlier murders, stories of violence. Whether they were true or not, in that moment, I believed anything was possible.

Rumors swirled that he had killed a friend of mine and his guest from the mainland with an axe or machete. And now he was here—at Lila Farm—right below me.

If I didn't act, they were going to die.

I jumped out of bed, yanked on my swim trunks, slipped into flip-flops, and ran up the hill to Jeff's house. In a complete panic, I shook him awake: "They're being killed—we have to go. Right now!"

Jeff didn't hesitate. He threw on some clothes, grabbed a flashlight, and we bolted back down toward the house.

At the driveway, a brand-new Jeep Cherokee was parked, aimed straight at the front door. Lights blazed inside, shadows moved, voices screamed. And when we looked inside the Jeep, our blood ran cold.

Inside the Jeep, we saw rifles and shotguns scattered across the seats and floor.

We were two terrified hippies with nothing but a flashlight. What could we possibly do? Still, I was desperate to distract whoever was inside, to buy my neighbors time.

I reached in, flipped on the headlights, and shouted with every ounce of authority I could muster:

"This is the Kona police! You're surrounded! Throw down your weapons and come out!"

It was insane. Completely reckless. But it worked.

The lights inside the house went dark. And in that blackout, the family leapt off the back veranda into the coffee trees and lava rock. How they escaped serious injury in the jump is a miracle. It was an 8-9 ft jump. In the chaos, they escaped to a neighbor's house and called the police.

That's when I realized he wasn't alone. Another man stepped out, just as dangerous, maybe worse.

The two men stepped onto the porch—one with a revolver, the other with a deer rifle. The headlights lit them up like a stage. And instead of fleeing, they walked calmly down the driveway, right into the headlight of the jeep, straight toward us.

Low voices. Cold eyes. Weapons raised.

Jeff and I shouted again, "Put down your weapons we have you surrounded," bluffing as hard as we could. But it didn't matter. They walked right up. Lowell smirked at Jeff, grabbed his flashlight, and sneered, "What are you gonna do—shoot me with this?"

With a laugh, he smashed Jeff across the face with his revolver, dropping him instantly into the ditch.

Jacob screamed at me not to move—but it was too late. I was already stepping forward when he raised the rifle, aimed it at my face, and pulled the trigger.

The flash was blinding. I dropped face-first into the dirt; certain my head had been blown apart. But when I reached up, my skull was intact. No blood. No wound.

I was alive.

It was an impossible shot to miss—just a couple of feet from my face, followed by a blinding flash. But where was the bullet? My invisible Friend had stepped in again. Always faithful. Never wavering. It seemed to me that—whether I believed or not—He, She, or whoever this Presence was didn't care. They just kept showing up. Decidedly, always there to help me.

The rage in Jacob's eyes grew darker. I staggered to my feet, and he looked visibly shocked. In desperation, he swung the rifle like a bat, smashing it across the side of my head. Dazed, I kept trying to stand until finally the stock of the heavy deer rifle splintered against my skull. Jeff later told me each blow sounded like a watermelon smashing on the ground.

By this time, I was sitting on the ground, drenched in blood, as if someone had upended a bucket over my head. My face was torn, my teeth loose, my lip hanging, and stars exploded inside my skull. He was seething. After breaking his rifle over my head, he stormed to the back of his Jeep, grabbed a 12-gauge shotgun, and loaded it.

Still cursing, he walked over, shoved the muzzle between my eyes, and growled, "Haole, I'm going to blow your head off!"

I looked up at him and said, "Why are you going to kill me? I'm no threat to you—you've already knocked me senseless."

His reply was chilling: "Because I hate you."

And in that surreal moment, a verse from the Bible Paul had given me came back—about knowing a tree by its fruit. Good tree, good fruit. Bad tree, bad fruit. And I thought: *This is bad fruit.*

As I sat there—broken, bleeding, certain I was about to die— my thoughts turned to Paul. I thought about how much Paul

Papoulias loved Jesus Christ. Funny, the things that run through your mind when you're facing death. I had come to Hawaii searching for union with cosmic consciousness, longing to return to some Edenic purity. And now, here I was—with a 12-gauge shotgun shoved between my eyes. Not Nirvana. Not enlightenment. Just a bad crime novel come to life. I was in a living hell.

Amazingly, right about then, Lonnie and Stretch—who had run off earlier after seeing we were about to be killed—changed their minds. And my friend Jeff, dazed but determined, came back down the road, walked up to where I was sitting in the dirt, and sat beside me. No words—just presence. In that moment, their message to these men was clear: If you're going to kill John, you'll have to kill all of us.

That kind of bravery was beyond anything I could have expected. They knew—without question—that these men were capable of murder. Yet they came anyway. Risked everything. It cracked something open in me. For the first time, I began to understand why God, despite all our rebellion and weakness, still holds humanity in such high regard. We matter. We're worth something.

What happened next felt like another intervention by my invisible Friend—stepping in once again to save me and my friends from what looked like certain death.

Somehow, instead of pulling the trigger, Jacob just continued to curse and tell me how much he hated me. And when it seemed certain we would all die, headlights and flashlights appeared—police pouring out of the banana trees with guns drawn.

The family was safe. My life—and my friends'—was spared.

But that night was far from over.

One of the attackers, Jacob, bolted into the banana grove and disappeared. For days he hid in the hills—at one point, in the storage shed beneath my very house. I slept above him, battered and broken, not even knowing he was there.

When the police finally caught him, I was left to face weeks of recovery. My body was shattered. But more than that, my illusions were gone.

This wasn't enlightenment. This was hell breaking loose in real time. And in the middle of it all, my invisible Friend remained —faithful, steady, never leaving.

I was severely injured—double concussions, skull fractures, and lacerations that required stitches. For over a month, I couldn't move my head or get out of bed without vomiting. I lost much of my balance and sense of direction for weeks.

While I was recovering, the police caught Jacob, and Lowell was already in jail. The police came to see me, asking if I'd be willing to testify at their trials. The police explained to me that no one had ever dared testify against this gang, for fear of retaliation.

But I was furious. What they had done to me—and what they had done to my friend and his guests just weeks before—was beyond anything I could excuse. So I said yes. I would testify in open court.

At first, they promised me protection. That didn't happen. I was on my own. I became the first person ever to testify against this mob, and the intimidation began immediately. Threats poured in—phone calls promising to blow up my house. Armed thugs showed up on my property, hunting for me.

Sometimes, when I heard their 4x4s coming through the trees, I'd climb into the macadamia nut trees in the pouring rain and stay hidden for hours. I'd watch them search around my house, weapons drawn. My heart pounded so hard I was afraid they could hear it.

Going to court was terrifying. The gang lined the courthouse steps—massive Hawaiian men blocking the entrance, growling, "Keep your mouth shut, haole. You're a dead man."

The fear was constant, suffocating. I slept with Teddy's 12-gauge on my pillow; every noise outside might have been my death sentence.

If you've never experienced that kind of fear—constant, suffocating, 24/7—it's hard to describe. I became a prisoner of intimidation. I slept with a 12-gauge shotgun on my pillow. A weapon that Teddy had loaned me. Every noise outside could mean death.

But eventually, the trial came. And the moment I stood in open court, pointed at those two men, and said, "Yes—those are the men who tried to kill me that night among the banana trees in Honaunau"—I felt something shift. It was terrifying. But it was also satisfying.

One of them was out on bail for a while. Later, word around town was that he'd been killed—people said it was an assassination. The other one was convicted of attempted murder—attempting to kill me—and sent to prison.

And I heard... while in prison, he became a believer in Jesus.

I actually felt compassion for him. In some ways, he was more of a victim than I was. He had grown up in a culture that stripped him of his proud Hawaiian heritage and offered him only sick counterfeits: drugs, violence, and the illusion of power. He'd been robbed—just like so many others.

I bore no hatred. Just heartbreak.

CHAPTER THIRTY-ONE
NOW WHAT?

After the trial—Lowell dead and Jacob in prison—I was left with one haunting question:

Now what?

I'd spent weeks healing from the beatings—painful, disorienting weeks where I didn't know which hurt worse: my body or my spirit. However, the good news was that I never heard from the gang again. Just being able to put the shotgun away, to walk out my front door without looking over my shoulder... that was a freedom most people take for granted. I didn't, not after what I'd lived through.

I went back to working in the garden, tending the bananas and harvesting avocados. But something was off. I was sad and flat. Maybe it was the head trauma, maybe not—but it was real. The joy was gone.

I had nothing in common with the Lila Farm crowd. The drugs didn't appeal to me. I drank less. I stopped partying. I had no interest in going backward. And while diving and surfing with my friends, Calvin and Claire, were the few bright spots in my week, it wasn't enough. I couldn't shake the feeling that this isn't it. There's more.

I say that—it wasn't enough—because it kept echoing through me. Something inside stirred—questions I couldn't answer kept rising. My life looked enviable from the outside. But inside, it was joyless. I was merely surviving, going through the motions.

The Pilgrims were becoming increasingly annoying. Not all of them, but those who tried to scare me into salvation. The ones who said I was going to hell unless I repented of my wickedness and made Jesus the "Lord of my life." I couldn't reconcile that with the One who had saved me again and again—the One I'd known since childhood. The One who used to meet me in my big oak tree when I was just a kid—the One who loved me so deeply when I felt completely unloved by the one person who was supposed to love me... my mother. Could that same One really be mad at me now? Would He really send me to a burning hell forever just for making the wrong choices?

No. I knew better.

That wasn't Him. That was a lie.

But there were others—the Pilgrims who said God (Jesus) loved me with no strings attached, that He cared for me. Period. No threats. No ultimatums. Just love.

And something in me started to wonder...

Could that One—the Rescuer, the Invisible Friend—really be Jesus?

I didn't have the answer yet.

But the question itself was relentless—driving me to find out.

CHAPTER THIRTY-TWO
MONCADO AND THE MASONS

After the trial, I needed work—and maybe some sense of normalcy. Jackie—the friend who had tragically lost his son in a home birth—told me that an elderly Filipino friend of his—Floral Sebai—was looking for help in his masonry business. I went to see Floral. He was in his seventies but full of energy, still running his masonry company and even a plantation back in the Philippines. He hired me on the spot as a hod carrier for his next job.

I was the youngest on the crew and was assigned to Cornelio as his helper. Cornelio, my assigned mason, was 82—Filipino with some Hawaiian blood, which made him taller and broader than the rest. The crew itself ranged from sixty-nine to a staggering 102 years old. We were working on the exterior stonework for a new supermarket in Captain Cook village. These men were incredible. They moved at what seemed like a snail's pace, but by the end of an eight-hour workday, their production was remarkable.

They were strict vegetarians. At lunch, they unpacked boiled peanuts, potatoes, and endless grape sodas—fuel enough, it seemed, to carry their wiry frames through another day of stonework. Most of them spoke Tagalog and broken English. Working alongside them was a powerful learning experience— their work ethic was unmatched. After a full day on the job, they'd head home to tend their own papaya or avocado farms.

They were deeply spiritual, always encouraging me to come to their church. But it never felt pushy. They spoke of Jesus with warmth and gentleness, never using fear or guilt to coerce me into going to church. Their kindness and honesty made an impression on me. Maybe, I thought, their brand of Christianity was worth giving a chance. It couldn't hurt to visit their church.

I had passed their church many times—it was a picture-perfect white chapel on a hill, complete with a bell tower, a cross, and beautifully cared-for grounds. I had grown disillusioned with the hippie and New Age culture, and I was starting to feel more sympathetic toward the claims of the Christians, though I still rejected the whole idea of a burning hell. If Jesus were who they claimed He was, then He'd have to speak to me personally. And honestly, I was becoming more open to the idea.

So finally, I gave in and attended the Filipino church in Captain Cook with my new Filipino friends. Floral introduced me to everyone as I entered. The church interior was neat and bright, with rows of wooden pews that quickly filled with a few dozen very elderly Filipino men and women. The whole congregation seemed genuinely excited to see me. I think Floral, an elder there, had told them I was coming.

Floral approached me and asked if I would be willing to read a scripture to the congregation. I felt uncomfortable with the request —I wasn't a Christian, and it felt strange to read the Bible out loud on my very first visit. But I reluctantly agreed. I don't remember what passage I read, but I do remember the large painting on the wall. It was a portrait of a man in full military uniform—with a third arm protruding from his tunic. At first, I thought I was seeing it wrong—but no, the painting really did show a third arm.

Below the painting was Isaiah 53:1: *To whom has the arm of the Lord been revealed?* And the name: General Moncado.

After I sat down, one of the church elders walked up front, pulled out an old 78 rpm record, and placed it on a record player. A scratchy, barely intelligible speech played over the speakers— apparently, a recording of General Moncado himself. They listened in rapt attention, not wanting to miss a word, even though the sound was nearly impossible to understand.

As it turns out, this sect had been playing copies of this exact speech wherever the Moncado Foundation met—from its origins in the Philippines to wherever its believers traveled.

Later, I learned he had served under General MacArthur in World War II and was a national hero in the Philippines. But to this group, he was more than a hero—they worshiped him as a prophet, maybe even the second coming of Christ.

To say I was dumbfounded and speechless would be an understatement. I had innocently agreed to attend church with Floral and the stone masons because I was curious and genuinely wanted to experience more of what Christianity had to offer. I had no idea they weren't Christians at all—but were actually worshiping a dead Filipino general.

As I sat there, still reeling, Floral came up to me and said they wanted to give me a blessing—something not many outsiders were invited to experience. He handed me a large book, saying it contained secret knowledge they guarded closely, but that he felt he could trust me with it. I opened it slowly... only to find page after page of Filipino men (not a single woman) posing in bathing suits—bodybuilding-style photos that seemed intended to show off the effects of their vegetarian diet and their supposed superior physical and spiritual health.

I was flabbergasted. I closed the book and handed it back without comment, doing my best to hide my shock. The last thing I wanted was to offend these kind, gentle, and sincere people.

I had really been trying to give this Christian thing a fair shot. But clearly, I had missed the mark wildly with this church.

Monday morning, back at work, Cornelio asked how I'd enjoyed the service. I had said nothing the day before, probably because I was still so stunned. I told him respectfully that I wouldn't be attending again—that it just wasn't what I was looking for.

Cornelio passed that along to Floral Sebai, who promptly called me over—and without any explanation, fired me on the spot.

I figured I'd have to keep looking for the truth. Anywhere but the Fellowship of Christian Pilgrims.

CHAPTER THIRTY-THREE
THE PRAYER IN THE DITCH

After I was fired by Floral Sebai, life on the farm just continued on as usual. I had isolated myself from most of my friends on the farm —the parties, drugs, and women were not for me—and I'd become a bit of a recluse in the midst of the craziness. I loved the people around me and recognized that they, like me, were simply trying to find purpose—to figure out what it meant to be alive and breathing on this planet.

I was just going through the motions of living, almost oblivious to the beauty and blessings that surrounded me. I'd somehow lost the wonder of being alive in such a physical, material paradise— and with it, the deep thankfulness that used to flow from that wonder. It wasn't just sadness. Some of it lingered from the head injuries. But deeper still, it was a weariness of soul.

It was December 1973. Looking back, I'd crammed an entire lifetime into those three years in Hawaii. Yet despite all my searching, all my experiences, I felt further than ever from the truth I was trying so hard to find.

Sadness settled in—a kind of quiet despair.

I still tended to my gardens—the bananas and coffee, which I loved—and I'd occasionally take my organic produce down to the Fellowship of Christian Pilgrims' store, the Manna Trading Co. I always looked forward to seeing my friend who worked the counter. Even though she was a "Pilgrim," there was something so real about the light she carried.

She spoke of a God named Jesus who lived inside us—in our innermost being—and talked to us constantly. She said He would never leave or abandon us, that we mattered to Him. That He created us. That we were the crown of His creation.

She never made me feel condemned or "less than." I couldn't say that about most of the other Christian zealots I'd met—the ones who insisted God would fry me like bacon if I didn't repent of my sin.

My experience with Floral Sebai and the Moncado Foundation had really shaken me. It left me emotionally raw. We were all just groping in the dark, trying to find answers. Questioning who we are and why we're here. Contrived answers that explained nothing.

I was sincere in wanting to explore whether Jesus Christ was the one who had been with me all along. I had already rejected the idea of some impersonal cosmic force that held both good and evil in balance—it just didn't line up with my own experiences. One by one, I was discarding the god concepts that didn't fit. After coming so close to death, I knew I had to glimpse behind the veil of this life —maybe for answers, maybe just to finally find myself.

One night, I was especially low. My car had broken down, so I decided to go for a walk to clear my head. I headed down the long driveway, leaving Lila Farm. It was dark, and a soft mist filled the air. The coolness of the evening felt good on my skin, and the sweet, powerful scent of wild yellow ginger surrounded me. Until you've stood among acres of it in full bloom, no description can really capture the smell—it was overwhelming, in the best way.

I was all alone with my thoughts on Christmas Eve, December 1973, walking from the farm's driveway toward Kuakini Highway. When I reached the road, I decided to keep going north, toward Kailua. A light rain was falling, and the mist hung low in the air. I had no destination in mind, just a need to walk.

I heard a pickup truck approaching from behind. They pulled over and asked if I wanted a lift—we were just a short distance from the Filipino Dance Hall, and you could already hear the music. I said, "Sure, why not?" I was just rambling, going nowhere in particular. I climbed into the back and sat on the edge of the truck bed, near the cab, my back to the road, my legs inside the truck bed. As we took off, the driver picked up speed until we were flying down the road. The misty rain and cool night air hitting my face felt invigorating.

My enjoyment of the ride was short-lived. Suddenly, the tires squealed, the truck slid sideways, and something slammed into my back so hard it knocked me face-down into the bed of the truck. I was in a daze—confused, disoriented, and not sure what had just happened. The pain in my spine was intense. Whatever hit me struck me hard—square in the middle of my back.

The truck stopped, now sitting sideways in the road. The silence and darkness were eerie. A guy jumped out and asked if I was okay. I got up slowly from the bed of the truck, dazed, and said, "My back hurts like hell! What happened?"

He screamed, "We hit a man! We hit a man in the road. Oh my God—we hit a man!"

I painfully climbed out of the truck. He told me the man we hit had gone flying through the air and landed in a ditch off the side of the road. As it turns out, he was an elderly, drunk Filipino walking in the dark and rain—right down the middle of the road—coming home from the Filipino Dance Hall. By the time the driver saw him, it was too late, and we had struck him.

Technically, the truck didn't hit him—I did. His head slammed into my back with such force it threw me face-first into the truck bed and hurled him into the ditch.

While the driver moved the truck out of the way and ran to a nearby house to call for an ambulance, I crossed the road and climbed down into the ditch. I found the man moaning in pain and crying that he didn't want to die—in broken English and, I assumed, Tagalog. His head had wedged into the crook of a tree, and his entire scalp was peeled off, hanging from the back of his neck. There was a lot of blood. It was a terrifying sight.

Carefully, I peeled the scalp from the back of his neck and laid it back over his head tucking it around the front above his eyebrows. I did what I could to comfort him, trying to reassure him that he wasn't going to die.

It was Christmas Eve, and somehow his drunken celebration had nearly killed us both.

I didn't want him to die. So I prayed—honest and desperate—hoping to make a deal.

"Jesus, if You are God like the Christians say, please save this poor man's life. Tomorrow is Christmas. If You let him live, I'll go to church on Christmas Day. But not the General Moncado church."

It wasn't a polished prayer—just a desperate bargain. Soon the ambulance came and rushed him to the hospital.

CHAPTER THIRTY-FOUR
A GREAT BIG CHRISTMAS PRESENT FROM JESUS

Christmas morning, December 25, 1973, I woke up early. It was hard to sleep—not just from the pain in my spine, but from worrying about the old Filipino man who'd collided with me the night before. The memories of that night were so surreal it was hard to believe they had actually happened. The pain in my back told me they had.

And then there was the prayer.

I had asked a God I wasn't even sure I believed in to save that man's life. It's amazing how intricately my life was about to become intertwined with whether or not he survived. What I didn't know then was that this day—this very Christmas morning—would change me and the course of my life forever.

My invisible, cosmic Friend had been at work all along—gently arranging the circumstances of my life to bring me to this moment. A moment that would finally begin to reveal His identity.

I got dressed and walked back down the same driveway I had walked the night before. When I reached Kuakini Highway, I stuck out my thumb. A car picked me up quickly and took me straight to Konawaena Hospital.

At the front desk, I asked if I could see the gentleman who had been brought in by ambulance the night before. They gave me a room number.

At least I knew he wasn't dead.

As I walked down the hallway, my thoughts ran wild. Was he paralyzed? Brain-damaged? Was he even conscious? I braced myself for anything.

To my amazement and joy, he was sitting up in bed eating breakfast.

The only visible evidence of the accident was a cast on his arm and a thick row of stitches running across his scalp—like something out of a Frankenstein movie. Relief washed over me. He had survived.

After a short visit, I left the hospital and sat down on the lawn out front. I remembered the prayer I had whispered in that ditch— the promise I had made to God.

I meant it.

I had told Him that if He saved the old man's life, I'd go to church on Christmas Day. And as strange as it was—after everything—I was fully committed to keeping that promise.

Thankfulness overwhelmed me. I couldn't explain it, but I knew my prayer had been heard, even answered. And in my heart, I felt that I was nearing the end of a long journey. All the roads, all the detours, all the wrong turns—they were starting to converge.

And it was all coming together on Christmas Day.

As I sat outside the hospital, I looked across the street and saw a little church. I knew the place—its pastor was a friend of mine. We both sold bananas and avocados through the local growers' co-op. I knew he was a Christian, and it seemed to me he genuinely lived what he believed. The church was called an Assembly of God. I didn't know what that meant, but I figured it couldn't be worse than the Moncado bunch.

I stood up and made my way across the street, determined to keep my word to the God I had prayed to. I wasn't sure what I was walking into—I just hoped it wouldn't leave me as disillusioned as the last church had.

I opened the front door, and even before I fully stepped inside, I could hear Brother Proferio preaching in Tagalog. It was an all-Filipino congregation, and the entire service was in the national language of the Philippines. I didn't understand a word.

I stepped inside the church—and instantly, my entire body was overtaken by something I can only describe as a tidal wave of love that knocked me off my feet. I lay there, saturated—overwhelmed by the love and power of God. There was no doubt in my mind—this was Jesus, embracing me with the supernatural love of His Spirit.

Human language doesn't have the words to describe this kind of revelation of God. I knew the love I was feeling wasn't just coming from the outside—it was welling up from deep inside of me. As I hit the floor, I'm sure anyone watching would've thought I was in pain, writhing around like I'd been hurt. But what I was experiencing was so deep, so overwhelming, that I wept and moaned and rolled on the floor as wave after wave of the love and glory of Jesus swept over me.

At last, my invisible Friend—the One who had been with me my entire life—revealed His name.

Jesus.

The relief I experienced was supernatural, and every doubt was destroyed. I didn't just realize I was forgiven—I knew I was being recreated as a new person, as He consumed my doubts with the pure, unadulterated love of God. It seemed like it lasted forever—me, sobbing and crying out loud on that church floor, allowing myself to be loved by the Lover of my soul. To be embraced like that... to feel as if you're being swallowed, consumed by Love itself—*that* changed me forever. I blinked, and I was a different man.

The One I had been so desperately seeking was made known to me that day. Jesus found me—His lost lamb, His prodigal son, finally home.

And I knew, without a doubt, that He hadn't just walked beside me. He had been living inside of me—gently guiding, directing, moving my life toward Himself.

As I lay on the floor in supernatural ecstasy, I could see the Cross of Christ. Suddenly, it became clear. The cross I had mocked and dismissed as a "bloody cross," the one I had laughed at and rejected, had now become the instrument of my healing, my knowing, my brand-new life. That Cross—His passion and love for me—had bought it all.

And His resurrection from the dead was being proven in me that very day... on the floor of the Assembly of God in Konawaena, Hawaii.

Gradually, the waves of glory began to recede. I became aware of four or five Filipino ladies kneeling beside me, their hands resting gently on me as they prayed in languages I knew weren't

Filipino. As they prayed, I started coming back to myself. The weeping subsided.

These women were so tender, so full of compassion, I felt like I was still being held in the embrace of Jesus. They helped me to my feet with such kindness that the love continued flowing through them. Brother Proferio stood nearby, grinning from ear to ear. I know that as both a friend and a pastor, he had prayed and hoped for this day.

The joy in that little church ran deep. They saw a brother step out of darkness and be born into the Kingdom of the Son, and they celebrated—loudly praising the Lord in Tagalog. I didn't understand a word, but their love for Jesus was unmistakable.

It's so strange how my life had become so intertwined with the Filipino community in Kona. Even the old drunk man I hit, and the promises I made to God that night, somehow led me into this tiny Filipino chapel. And this—this—was the place where Jesus, my invisible Friend, finally revealed His identity to me.

So many years. So many paths I had walked on this long journey. But now I could see the Cross clearly—how He gave everything so I could have this new life.

I knew Him now. Alive. Resurrected from the grave. Living in me. I was in Him, and He was in me.

But deep down, I also knew this was just the beginning. A new adventure had begun—walking with my Friend, Jesus.

As miraculous and unforgettable as this day was, compared to what would unfold over the next fifty years, it was only the beginning.

CHAPTER THIRTY-FIVE

FOUND BY CHRIST

I left Brother Proferio's church and hitched a ride back to Lila Farm. I was in an emotional and spiritual state that could only be described as *blissed out*. There was a joy so deep in my soul—a sense of satisfaction and pleasure that words can't fully capture.

For the first time in my life, I knew who my invisible Friend was—Jesus Christ, God's Son.

As I walked up—no, danced—joyfully up the driveway toward my house, I stopped by Teddy's place on the way up the hill and blurted out the news to my neighbors.

"I've been found by Christ. I'm saved!"

They were shocked to hear the good news. Vivian looked stunned. Later, she would come to know the Great Shepherd and join the Pilgrims.

Next, I headed to Lonnie's house. I walked right in and announced to Lonnie, his wife Alesia, Jeff, and Stretch:

"I've personally met Jesus—and I'm a different man."

They looked at me and chuckled. It was clear they had *no* idea what I was talking about. I didn't even try to explain it. They probably thought I was on drugs or something.

I made my way over to my own house and just basked in the glory of God.

Jesus Christ loves me—He loved me first. I was lost, and He found me. And I love Him so much. A joy beyond words had filled my soul.

The deep depression that had weighed me down was gone— lifted in an instant.

I was happy—even though I was still doing the same things I had done before meeting Jesus, everything felt different now. I wasn't merely surviving anymore—I was truly alive. Gratitude filled my heart for even the smallest things. I could see the loving hand of God everywhere.

The Kona coast radiated the love of the Father for His creation. It was unmistakable. In the deep blue Pacific Ocean... the glorious parade of flowers and fruit trees in every imaginable color... the songs of birds, the warmth of the sun, the sound of waves breaking on the shore—He was present in all of it.

It's amazing what you see when your eyes finally open to reality.

I didn't really know what I was going to do now.

I just knew I needed to be around people who had experienced what I had—people who actually knew the real truth about the love of God. I sensed that some of the Pilgrims knew the same Jesus I had encountered.

I didn't avoid them as carefully anymore.

I kept talking with the ones who didn't try to threaten me with hellfire if I didn't do what *they* said I had to do to know Jesus.

I had lost my job working with Floral Sebai as an apprentice mason, so I knew I had to look for work.

A couple of Christians told me the Kona Surf Hotel was hiring kitchen help, so I applied for a job as fifth cook. When they asked about my qualifications, I explained that my family had owned a small restaurant when I was a teenager and I had worked in all phases of it. They hired me on the spot and put me right to work—with multiple job assignments.

My shift started at 3:00 a.m. and went until 11:00 a.m. Since I didn't have a car, I had to leave home before 2:00 a.m. and ride my bike about seventeen miles—mostly downhill—to the hotel.

I flew through the cool night air, past acres of yellow ginger and fragrant gardenias. The scent was so powerful it was almost intoxicating—like breathing in a living bouquet. I loved that ride. It was quiet and still, just the rush of wind past my face and the soft swoosh of my bike tires on the pavement. I felt so close to the One who loved me. I could sense His presence all around me in the darkness.

My first task in the kitchen was helping the baker prepare the day's cakes, pies, and pastries. As the morning went on, I'd help with the salads and food prep for the massive lunch buffets that fed the busloads of tourists arriving daily to experience Hawaiian aloha.

I really liked that job. And it gave me the chance to tell anyone who'd listen that Jesus loved them.

By February of 1974, I realized I couldn't keep living at Lila Farm. I loved everyone there deeply—these were people I had shared so much of life with—but our paths had diverged so dramatically that I knew it was time to move on. There was no judgment in my heart toward those who had been my closest friends for years. They were still *my people*. But after what I had experienced, there was no longer any common ground.

In March, I received a letter from the state of Hawaii asking if I'd be willing to come to the state offices in Hilo for a meeting with some officials.

The letter said it was regarding a new law that had recently passed—something called the "Good Samaritan Law." Apparently, a detective from the Kona Police Department had given them my name. That's all I knew.

We set a date, and I caught a ride over to Hilo for the meeting. When I walked into the office, several officials and the detective who had submitted my name were seated around a table. I sat down, still unsure what this was about.

They began by explaining that I was one of the first people being considered for a reward under the new law. The detective had told them about what happened about the night at the banana grove—how, by distracting the attackers, the family escaped and called the police.

As the meeting continued, they informed me that I would be awarded $1,400 under the provisions of the Good Samaritan Law.

I was stunned. I had no idea that's what the meeting was about. I had only done what any neighbor should do in a crisis. But the state had decided to honor me for it—and that meant more than I could say.

I was desperate to find like-minded believers—someone I could talk to, someone who could help me understand what came next in this new life I was experiencing. I needed guidance. Encouragement. Fellowship.

But there weren't many options.

If I wanted to talk to Christians, chances were it would be the

Pilgrims. They were everywhere. A lot of my friends—and hundreds of hippies—had left behind their freak lifestyles and crumbling communes to join the Fellowship of Christian Pilgrims.

I started up conversations with a few Pilgrims I knew and liked. I was still a little suspicious of the whole movement, but I was getting desperate for Christian friendship.

During one of those chats, someone told me about a Christian rock concert coming up at Hale Hālāwai, a concert venue in downtown Kailua. A band called *The Way* was going to perform.

They encouraged me to go. I wasn't so sure.

A *Christian rock concert*? That sounded completely absurd to me. But I wasn't exactly in the loop when it came to the Christian scene—and curiosity got the better of me.

I drank a little wine and brought a non-Christian friend with me that evening. But as soon as we walked into the venue, he turned around and left—refusing to go in. I guess he was spooked by the hundreds of people gathered to hear the music. (Christian Pilgrims *were* kind of frightening to the freaks in Kona.)

I stayed.

I pushed through the crowd, working my way to the front. I told myself I didn't want to miss anything that might help me understand what had happened to me.

I stood right at the edge of the stage, surrounded by people, waiting in anticipation. The band came out and immediately launched into a song called *He's the Reason to Go On.*

Almost instantly, I felt the same Spirit I had experienced at the Filipino church. As they played, I was overwhelmed by the love of God—and again, I fell to the floor, weeping, loudly crying. Right there. Right in front of hundreds of Pilgrims. I was making a complete spectacle of myself.

The lead guitarist stepped off the stage, knelt down, helped me up, and asked, "What do you need?"

I sobbed, "I don't know what I want... but I want what you have."

The people around me laid their hands on me, and the guitarist prayed. I felt like I was being filled to overflowing with the love of God. It poured out of every pore in my body.

And I knew who it was.

It was Jesus. Unmistakably, undeniably—my Friend.

So many of the people there that night knew who I was. They knew how I had gone out of my way for years to be obnoxious and unkind to the Pilgrims. But none of that mattered anymore. They rejoiced—because the prodigal had come home.

Yes, Jesus had seen me coming from far off. And He ran to meet me. He threw His best coat over my shoulders, placed a ring on my finger, a crown on my head, and threw a party.

Because His son had come home.

I talked with the band after the concert. They were all happy teenagers from Southern California, full of joy, and they gave me a copy of their album.

I was overwhelmed—intoxicated, but not from the small glass of wine I'd had earlier. No, I was smashed. Intoxicated in the Holy Spirit of God.

It was late when I finally left the venue. I was so dazed, so undone, I wandered straight into oncoming traffic—to the sound of honking horns and screeching tires.

I made it home safely—more determined than ever to leave Lila Farm.

EPILOGUE

In my wildest dreams, I never would've thought I'd even *consider* becoming a Pilgrim.

There were so many reasons I couldn't.

The biggest one? The belief held by many of them in eternal punishment—a burning hell for not believing the gospel *their* way, or for rebelling in some form. That alone had always kept me far away.

But I'd met enough believers in the Fellowship of Christian Pilgrims who didn't hold to that doctrine, and I knew I could learn a lot from being in fellowship with other believers.

So I went and talked to the two young guys who had invited me to the concert and asked if it might be possible to live in one of the community houses. They told me there was plenty of space— over thirty fellowship houses scattered along the Kona coast. They directed me to the Pilgrims Inn, the main meeting house of the fellowship. It was a converted hotel with two residential wings—

one for brothers and one for sisters—connected by a central building with a meeting hall and commercial kitchen.

I was nervous. I didn't really know what I was getting myself into.

But I was willing to give the Pilgrims an honest try.

I walked up to one of the doors and knocked.

A young man answered. He looked like the Fonz—black motorcycle jacket, greased-back hair, chewing gum, and a tough-guy expression. He gave me a once-over with what I felt was a smart-ass smirk and said, "If you want to live here, you have to submit."

Not exactly the warm welcome I had hoped for.

Ordinarily, I would've told him to F-off and walked away. I had always been a rebel. And the word *submit*? That was one I *hated*.

But before I could say a word, I heard a voice—clear and direct —on the inside:

"John, just shut up and do what the man says."

So I did.

I agreed to his terms. He showed me to the room I'd be staying in and introduced me to my new roommate, David Smith. I thanked him and left the Inn to head back to the Farm and gather my things.

I walked into Lonnie's house and told him what had happened at the concert. I gave him the band's vinyl album and shared how Jesus had revealed Himself to me—how I was now a Christian, a part of God's growing family—a new man. The old life was gone.

Jeff and Stretch were there too. They laughed and said, "Don't worry, John, you're just on another of your weird trips. Give it time —you'll come out of it."

They thought it was a joke.

But when I told them I was leaving the Farm to move into the Pilgrims Inn, they were stunned. Becoming a Pilgrim had always been a running joke around the Farm. They couldn't wrap their heads around the fact that I was serious.

I went to my little house and packed up the few things I owned.

Then I walked up the hill to where my pot plants were growing and pulled them out of the ground.

A few months earlier, my friend Cal and I had hiked up the mountain to catch some wild baby piglets. When we got them home, we put them in a pen to fatten them up for a luau in the *imu* pit. The reason I share this is because of what I did next.

As I carried the pot plants down to the pigpen, a few people gathered and pleaded with me:

"Don't waste the pot, John—give it to us!"

But I wouldn't be deterred.

I threw every last plant into the pigpen.

The piglets immediately started eating them.

I was closing a chapter in my life.

And it felt so good.

I got a ride down to the Pilgrims Inn and unloaded my stuff from the car.

I stood there for a moment—just staring at the building.

I could hardly believe it.

I was becoming a Pilgrim.

What was I doing?

I was hoping that voice I'd heard—that instruction to shut up and do what the man said—was really God. I was about to find out.

I didn't know what would happen next. I just knew I wasn't

the same man who came to the Big Island chasing a dream—because the dream found me.

After Father, Son, and Spirit's self-revelation in Christ, the beauty of the natural world is magnified and increases as we gaze upon His Masterpiece and have a divine awareness that it was created for Us, the very Crown of His Creation.....

John Land
always a son.

ABOUT THE AUTHOR

John Land, a San Francisco Bay Area native and baby boomer, served four years as a medical specialist in the U.S. Air Force. After serving in Japan, he returned to a transformed San Francisco, captivated by the psychedelic counterculture. Immersed in the movement, he explored Buddhism, eastern mysticism, and the use of psychedelics for spiritual enlightenment, inspired by Timothy Leary's philosophy.

Years later, John discovered that the love of God was the answer he had been seeking. With his wife Lois, he has dedicated over forty years to serving the needy through their non-profit, Christian Outreach Resource Endeavor (CORE), providing essential aid in Baja, Mexico, and Lebanon to war-torn Syrian refugees. John's memoir offers a firsthand account of his journey, shedding light on a generation's pursuit of meaning and the profound impact of unconditional love.

ABOUT THE PUBLISHER

Discover more from TWS Publishing—our authors, their books, and more—at:

www.thewriterssocietypublishing.com

Made in the USA
Middletown, DE
23 November 2025

21144651R00130